UPCYCLING
WITH STYLE

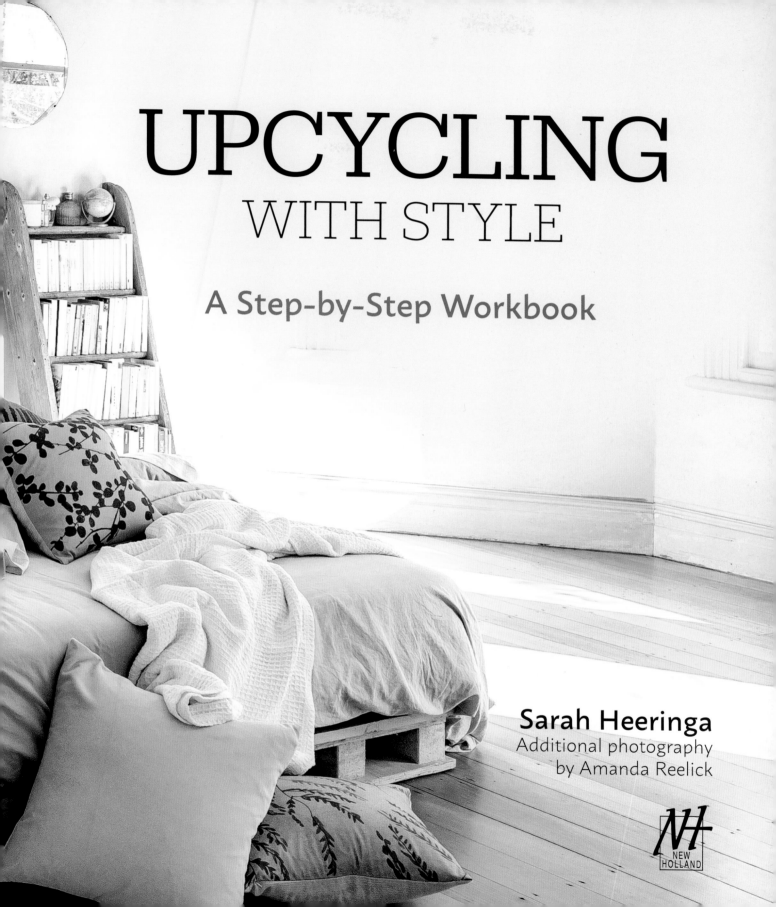

UPCYCLING
WITH STYLE

A Step-by-Step Workbook

Sarah Heeringa
Additional photography
by Amanda Reelick

NH
NEW
HOLLAND

To Vincent, for encouragement and humour in the face of all my creative endeavours.

Contents

INTRODUCTION

Home is where we begin and, for better or worse, our experience of home can fundamentally shape our outlook on life. What happens at home matters. A happy and functioning home is a goal well worth pursuing – it provides a private retreat from the world, a place to love and nurture our families, a setting in which we can explore our creativity, and somewhere we can welcome and enjoy the company of others.

What makes a house feel like a home?

It is human nature to want a place where we belong, but homeliness can be surprisingly hard to define as its physical expression can vary widely according to personal taste. It is as much about a home's atmosphere as it is about particular style trends or interior design.

Clean, dry and well-lit rooms are a good place to start, but that delicious feeling of home as haven tends to come from more intangible things: privacy, comfort and having personal items around that convey feelings of sentiment, genuine connection and meaning.

Our home feels like home to us partly because it blurs the line between us and our surroundings. Homeliness is lying in a sunny nook cuddling the cat. It can be found in home-cooked food and other handmade or personal comforts.

It lingers in family photos on the walls and music in the air, and it can be conjured in moments of laughter and conversation around a table. The point is, you don't need a dining table or a cluster of couches to have a conversation, but they help. This interplay between life and stuff is what makes interior design such a fascinating discipline.

I'm keen to keep learning, but I'm not much for mimicking interior design trends. I tend to think it is much more interesting if you can follow your own instincts rather than the fickle whims of fashion.

Naturally, we are all influenced by our surroundings, but simply buying into whatever is the in trend at any moment suggests a possible lack of imagination and contributes to our current culture of overconsumption and throw-away-ism.

It seems to me that the most interesting and welcoming homes are not made merely through shopping. Creating a home with personal style and a feel-good vibe is not achieved by slavishly following fashion trends.

Ultimately, it's more satisfying and the result is going to be more authentic if we can arrive at our own decisions about what we like and how we are going to go about furnishing the spaces where we live.

In the days before mass production everything was handmade and extremely intensive, and most people had relatively little choice about the objects they used to furnish their homes.

These days, globalisation and the abundance of cheap consumer goods means we have more choice than ever before about what to put in our homes. The question remains as to how we decide what items we choose and what we reject.

Creating a home that suits you and your family takes imagination and confidence. If you are like me, it will also take time as

The most interesting and welcoming homes are not made merely through shopping. Creating a home with personal style and a feel-good vibe is not achieved by slavishly following fashion trends. Ultimately, it's more satisfying and the result is going to be more authentic if we can arrive at our own decisions about what we like and how we are going to furnish the spaces where we live.

Our lives are a series of stories, told in part by the things we have around us.

you try various things, and involve learning from mistakes along the way.

Upcycling involves taking unwanted objects and giving them a new life – aiming to turn them into an item of use or beauty. One of the brilliant aspects of working with second-hand furniture and materials is that it gives you great freedom to experiment and try something new.

Paint is one of my favourite ways to change the look of an item and give it a new life, partly because it's relatively quick and easy, but also because it's so liberating.

There are hundreds of paint shades and tones to choose from. The creative challenge is picking the colour that effects the change you are after.

The dwelling you currently live in might be far from your dream home, but even on a limited budget there are simple things we can do to improve our surroundings. Decluttering, for instance, costs nothing but time and energy and can make a huge difference to the feel and functionality of a space.

Decluttering can be surprisingly difficult, but is usually well worth the effort – not to mention the satisfaction of dropping off a pile of surplus items to your local second-hand store.

Upcycling is almost the opposite of decluttering. It typically involves collecting tools and materials – at times with only a vague idea of how you're going to use them.

The urge to upcycle can see you bringing

odd things home from second-hand shops and collecting things from the side of the road or even out of skips.

But the result of a completed upcycling project can be just as satisfying as decluttering – and the cumulative effect of several projects in a room can be just as transformative.

There are many good reasons to upcycle. It saves timber, metal, fabric and other valuable resources from going into landfill. It helps you to unleash your creativity and learn new skills. It's a way to furnish our homes with quality items for a fraction of the cost of buying them new.

Upcycling means having things around us that have more significance than if we'd just bought them. And upcycling is also deliciously countercultural – allowing you to enjoy lovely things while side-stepping consumerism and throw-away-ism.

Upcycling is not quite the opposite of decluttering, because it so neatly complements it. The point of decluttering is to simplify our possessions, eliminating the unnecessary to make room for the

necessary and more useful. Upcycling, on the other hand, helps us to make more of our possessions by transforming the unnecessary and by making the necessary more beautiful.

This is my second book sharing ideas and practical tips for undertaking upcycling projects and for developing your own style. My first book on the topic was called *Reclaim That: Upcycling your home with style*.

I hope you find this new book inspiring and the projects fun to try as you curate a welcoming and personalised home for yourself and your family. It will be a home you won't see in a shopping catalogue because it's something far better – a home that is uniquely yours.

CHAPTER 1

GETTING STARTED

A simple item of furniture, such as an old chair, is a great upcycling project to get started with. If you choose something old and unwanted it will allow you even greater freedom to give things a go, make mistakes and learn new skills along the way.

You don't need a workshop stocked with specialist equipment to start upcycling. It is amazing what can be achieved with a few simple tools such as sharp scissors, sewing needle and cotton, or a handsaw, hammer and set of screwdrivers.

A bit of know-how can make things more doable than you might have imagined. Like how you can strip stain from wood just using old cloths, water, sugar soap and the kind of stainless steel scourer you might use to scrub the pots.

Sometimes things just need a really good clean before they can be repurposed. A lot can be achieved using a scrubbing brush and a bucket of warm soapy water. If you attach a spray gun fitting to a regular garden hose it turns into a water blaster of sorts that you can use to great effect.

When an item of furniture is broken a few key tools can make the challenge of mending or modifying less frustrating. And simple things such as figuring out the best glue to use in different situations can make or break a project.

A sewing machine is an outlay that

repays itself many times over when you can use it to mend torn items, and make or modify soft furnishings such as curtains, cushions and throws.

Charity stores and second-hand shops are an endless source of treasures and they can also be a great place to find quality old tools and useful pieces of fabric. Second-hand stores are a good source of jars, large pans and other preserving equipment.

Other useful tools to collect include pointy and snub-nosed metal pliers, large and small hammers and screwdrivers in a range of sizes and styles, including Phillips, flat and square heads of varying sizes.

The best screwdrivers and hammers are made with quality steel and have handles that are comfortable to grip. A few short-handled screwdrivers are also ideal for using inside awkward furniture corners.

Square-head screwdrivers and self-tapping square screws are an inspired invention. The screw fits snug on the screwdriver and drills its own hole as it is screwed in. They are easy to tighten and undo again.

Second-hand woodworking tools are often made with better quality steel than their modern equivalents and their smooth

Treasures to discover at Junk and Disorderly, junkndisorderly.co.nz

wooden handles have a lovely time-worn quality. G-clamps are very useful for gluing wood, metal and other such items together. Planes, rasps and files are also all used in woodwork and, like G-clamps, are the kind of tools that are worth looking out for at garage sales.

If you are gearing up to do re-upholstering you may want to invest in a powerful staple gun. But a lot can also be done with a hammer and tacks. Borer treatments need to be used with care but can protect infected wood from futher damage.

The fastest and most effective way to transform an item is often with paint, and old furniture provides the perfect opportunity to play around with paint effects and colour combinations. It is worth investing in quality paint products for long-lasting results. Also, look for paint brands with environmental credentials certified by an independent third party and offering VOC-free and low-VOC products. Volatile organic compounds (VOCs) emit toxic gasses, so are best avoided.

Paint brushes can be used multiple times if cleaned well after every use. It took me a while to figure this out and I ruined plenty of brushes in the meantime. I find the easiest and most eco-friendly method is to wash them out over grass using a garden hose fitted with a high-pressure nozzle.

A small, ergonomically shaped sander can quickly become an indispensable tool for

removing paint, smoothing surfaces and adding finishing touches to your upcycling projects.

As you embark on more ambitious upcycling projects, the range of power tools you want will likely grow. Serious tools

One simple pleasure of working on upcycling projects can be the familiar and tactile qualities of favourite tools – new and old.

such as drop saws, circular saws, jigsaws and electric grinders can be essential at times for projects requiring some degree of carpentry or construction.

Powerful tools take a bit of care and expertise to operate safely and are best used with earmuffs and safety goggles.

Try to avoid cheaply made gear when buying new. Choosing recognised brands does not guarantee quality but it is one place to start. Roughly cast plastic can be a clue things have not been well made. Lightness of weight can also be an indicator of poor grade steel, but in power tools, lightness is sometimes a sign of quality. It is great to find a store with hardware staff who will take you through the options.

Online reviews are also a good source of product information.

As you explore upcycling, some tools will become favourites you go back to using time and time again.

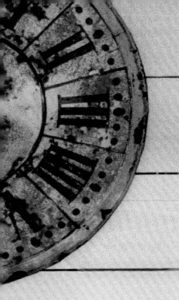

CHAPTER 2

FURNITURE FINDS

If you see a classic piece of furniture you like for sale in a high end store, chances are that if you go hunting with a bit of determination you will be able to find something similar second-hand.

There is a huge range of quality vintage and second-hand furniture on offer at charity stores, garage sales and online. And when you have an eye to the upcycling potential of things, you can see possible projects everywhere.

The challenge for the upcycler is not so much in finding furniture to bring home but in deciding what design style you like most.

There's a veritable smorgasbord of possibilities to choose from: modern rustic, coastal or nautical, Scandinavian, modernist, vintage, industrial, French country, modern Victorian, early settlers, midcentury modern or bohemian modern, to name just a few.

One way to go is to choose a distinct style and endeavour to apply it consistently across the board. An obvious advantage is that you will be able to achieve a very consistent look.

Or you may feel more comfortable with taking a looser approach, mixing styles and eras together. Often described as eclectic, this method intentionally uses a varied mix of pieces both old and new, and across a range of eras and décor trends. The goal is to combine it together in a cohesive whole and to create a space unique to you.

The choice is yours; after all, home is where you get to decide what you have around.

Furnishing a home is much like choosing what to wear – there are well-recognised classics, but beyond that pretty much anything goes. Ultimately it comes down to our own tastes as to what look we choose and are confident embracing and making work for us.

One of the liberating things about buying second-hand is that, as with op-shopping for clothes, picking up pieces at low prices allows plenty of opportunities for discovery and experimentation with many and various styles. And as an upcycler, if you find an item of furniture that is not quite right, you can always modify it to suit.

Alternatively, you can use a piece of furniture as raw materials to turn into something else by, for instance, taking a wooden headboard and making a tabletop.

Combining contrasting styles and textures can give your home a richness and a depth that rooms kitted out in matching furniture don't have. But you do need to apply a critical eye and some aesthetic discipline to avoid the final effect looking like an incoherent jumble.

A few simple techniques can help you achieve this. For instance, if you are mixing two noticeably different styles together, aim to space the pieces evenly across the room.

Another device is to use a consistent colour across several differently shaped items to create visual calm and to help aspects of the décor hang together.

Size matters; a mix of pieces from different eras will look more complementary if you keep the scale in the same realm. Or choose pieces that are basically matching in their lines and shapes, or include two of the same pieces of furniture. For example, if you are collecting mismatched chairs to go around a dining table, consider painting them all the same colour or having three sets of two different styles of chair.

Repairing an item or giving it a new look is a great skill to cultivate and can be hugely satisfying. Along the way we can develop our aesthetic eye, by paying attention to textures and fabrics and by learning to recognise the iconic colours, décor styles and designs of each decade.

It can all start with the decision to leave the mall and the main street behind and go hunting out the much more interesting and rewarding finds to be had in boutique, antique and second-hand stores.

Furnishing a home is much like choosing what to wear – there are well-recognised classics, but beyond that pretty much anything goes. Ultimately it comes down to our taste and confidence to run with it.

A scruffy but sound chair is a good project to start with if you are new to upcycling. Small occasional chairs such as this one are easy to paint or recover as the fancy takes you.

They do not require specialist tools or much in the way of materials, making them ideal to experiment on. All you need is paint, fabric, tacks, a small hammer and carpenter's glue to effect a transformation.

This little old chair has a slightly theatrical air, with some features of a classic Louis XVI dining chair, including a round, slightly reclined back and no connecting parts between the legs.

The chair's backrest had previously been painted gold but had become worn and chipped over time.

The chair has since been repainted with a grey-based metallic paint effect.

Over time it has had a number of different seat coverings, including having its leather seat painted blue, recovered in fake fur (see page 90) and recovered again in a striped taffeta with fringe trim.

See pages 248-250 for project notes.

BASIC CARVER CHAIR RE-FASHIONED

A chair might look very shabby but still be fundamentally sound. The simplest test of any chair is to sit in it and check if the seat creaks or the legs wobble.

You can turn a chair over to see how its joints have been constructed and if they are still firm. When turned over you can also look for a manufacturer's label or other clues as to the chair's age and provenance. Notice if old tacks or new staples have been used and if the backing is hessian or a more modern fabric.

If any joints are broken or have worked loose over time, the best way to make a lasting repair is to take the joints apart and re-glue them. You might need to add new dowels in the process. If you have G-clamps they can be very useful for a task like this.

Some old chairs, such as the one pictured right, can look bad but still be straight and firm.

This chair is in the style of a basic colonial carver chair. A chair like this can be used at the end of a dining table or as an occasional chair in a hall, lounge or bedroom.

One feature typical of a carver is the lack of vertical spindles between the armrest and the seat. Another is the three vertical supporting spindles on the chair back. Often the spindles on legs and armrests are turned on a lathe. Our basic carver only has turned spindles on the uprights of the armrests.

MATERIALS USED

Small claw hammer, screwdriver or pliers, drop cloth, paint brush, Resene Quick Dry Primer Undercoat, waterborne enamel paint, sandable filler, light sandpaper, sponge rubber squab, tape measure, fake fur, scissors, approximately 20 cut tacks.

STEP ONE

Use a screwdriver or pliers to lever up any old tacks and to remove the remains of old upholstery fabric.

A small claw hammer can be used to loosen and remove any small tacks. Or they can be tapped down flat.

STEP TWO

Wipe the chair free of dust and undercoat the arms, legs and back. Allow to dry. If undercoating has highlighted any small dents in the chair, fill with sandable filler. Once dry, sand smooth, including any paint dribbles.

STEP THREE

Topcoat with waterborne enamel. For a lighter, modern look I chose a soft grey tone.

STEP FOUR

An easy recovering option is to use a thick pile textile such as fake fur.

Cut a piece of sponge rubber to shape. Put the sponge in place on the chair and measure the area to recover from front to back and side to side.

Turn the fur over and mark the shape to cut on the back. Cut the fur while it is laid out this way, snipping though the hide or backing fabric but not cutting the fibers.

STEP FIVE

Starting at front and centre, fix the fur in place by tapping in tacks. On each side work from the middle out to the edges. Cut extra fabric from the corners as required. See pages 248-250 for project notes.

PAINTED HIGH BACK CHAIR

Below: This chair was craft-bombed by a group of women for a mutual friend, incorporating maps, fabric scraps and other significant mementos into the chair.

This snug armchair doesn't have wings but its high back and sides locate it in the wingback chair family.

Classic wingbacks were first made in England in the 1600s as fireside chairs. Their high backs were designed to protect a person's back from drafts and to trap any heat radiating from the fireplace. Side wings added extra draught blockers – perfect for chilly evenings in that draughty old mansion.

Our old blue armchair has compact proportions, making it ideal for a lounge corner, but it was very faded and needing a revamp. Fortunately, the chair's smooth surface and tightly-woven fabric make it ideal to paint.

Paint tends to seep through the threads of loosely woven fabric before it dries, but a tighter weave can easily be covered with a thin paint coating that remains flexible.

A coat in a deep blue took the chair from frumpy to fabulous.

MATERIALS USED

Drop cloth, paint brush, black paint for the feet and deep grey/blue for the chair.

See pages 248-250 for project notes.

LITTLE
STOOL RE-
UPHOLSTERED

Upgrading old upholstery is a sure way to breathe new life into furniture.

Some pieces are technically difficult and require the help of professionals to achieve the transformation you are after. Other items, such as this cute but shabby step stool, are more straightforward.

Look for a stool that is pleasingly shaped, made with solid wood or quality metal, and has sturdy legs and no borer. Consider how you might use the stool.

A step stool is best upholstered with firm padding and leather, vinyl or other hard-wearing, closely woven, stain-resistant fabric.

A lounge footstool could have softer fabric and padding. Either way, the quantities of fabric involved mean you can often use store remnants.

MATERIALS USED

To strip the stool: sugar soap, newspaper or drop cloth, rubber gloves, old cloths, stainless steel scourer.

To recover the stool: upholstery fabric, padding (sponge or woollen fabric), scissors, small hammer, 4 x flat-head tacks, 25 x upholstery tacks, scraper or flat-head screwdriver (optional).

STEP ONE

Use sharp scissors to snip away the top layer of the original fabric. Only remove as much as you must, as some original padding may be good enough to re-use.

Remove old staples and tacks by placing the flat edge of a scraper or flat-head screwdriver under an edge of the staple or tack. Tap the handle gently with a hammer.

If they are totally rusted in place you can simply cover them over with fabric.

STEP TWO

While the fabric covering is removed, you can sand and repaint the woodwork, or strip back any dark stain for a lighter look. Use the liquid cleaner sugar soap for this. For more on sugar soap see page 45.

STEP THREE

Cut padding to size. Sponge rubber can be used or for a firmer effect, or use layers of fabric, such as a woollen blanket.

STEP FOUR

Measure the top of the stool. Cut a new piece of fabric to cover the padding, allowing enough fabric on each side to turn it over by at least 2cm on each side.

If the fabric is likely to fray, zigzag around the edge. Iron the fabric fold flat along all four edges.

STEP FIVE

Lay the stool on its side and place one folded edge of the fabric over the padding and, starting from the centre, secure the fabric in place using the tacks.

Push each tack into place with your thumb and tap down using a hammer. Turn the stool over and repeat on the opposite side.

STEP SIX

Shape each corner by folding one edge of the fabric in, then the other. Tack the first fold in place using a regular flat-head tack, before covering it with the second fabric fold. Secure the corner fold using a furniture tack.

Tap all remaining tacks firmly into place to complete the project.

MID-CENTURY MODERN MAKEOVER

Mid-century modern was in vogue from the 1950s to the 1970s, and remains popular today. The design style is known for clean lines, smooth curved edges and lack of adornment or fancy upholstery. Thin, tapered or spiky legs made with wood or metal and set on an angle are another characteristic feature.

The style is likely to be trendy for a while yet. The designs suit modern apartments' small spaces and incorporate classic shapes.

The design style is easily recognised due to the many knockoffs. Replica Herman Miller Eames dining chairs (opposite) are one common example.

Look out for retro originals at charity stores and garage sales as you might find a treasure. Or give a nondescript item, such as this bookshelf (below), a mid-century modern makeover.

Tapered wooden legs can be handmade using a lathe or bought online, either second-hand or new. I salvaged a set of screw-in legs from an old broken sofa, including the original bits of frame with the angled threads. These were attached to the bottom of the shelf. A two-tone pastel paint finish completes the look.

See pages 248-250 for project notes.

Judging by the holes and marks along the back, this antique wooden sideboard once had shelves, making it a buffet hutch.

As with many vintage wooden pieces, this old sideboard was covered in a dark brown stain, which obscured any wood grain and contributed to its dull and dowdy appearance.

Various woods age differently over time. It also depends on what they have been stained with and how much sunlight they are exposed to. Mahogany and cherry timbers typically grow darker over time, while walnut can become lighter.

The least toxic way to remove an old stain is with a sugar soap solution and some vigorous scrubbing.

Sugar soap is a liquid household cleaner that is often used to prepare surfaces for painting. The same qualities that make it a powerful grease stripper also make it effective for lightening wood stains.

MATERIALS USED

To strip the cabinet: sugar soap, drop cloths or newspaper, metal bowl, rubber gloves, stainless steel scourer, cloths, bucket, old toothbrush.

To embellish the cabinet: gold paint and paint brush or aerosol, masking tape, natural furniture wax.

In making something usable from the unwanted
we retrieve something previously lost.

STEP ONE

Dilute the sugar soap by half with water.

Lay out a drop cloth or newspapers and put on gloves before evenly coating all stained surfaces with the solution.

Leave this solution to soak in for at least 10 minutes.

STEP TWO

While using gloves, scrub all surfaces vigorously using a stainless steel scourer. Use an old toothbrush to work into the corners.

After scrubbing an area wipe the wood surface clean with damp cloths repeatedly rinsed out in warm water. Work area by area.

Tip the waste sugar soap water on grass rather than down the drain to avoid harming marine life. Allow the timber to fully dry.

STEP THREE

Repeat steps 1 and 2, as necessary, to lift the stain. Apply spot scrubbing to get rid of any sugar soap dribble marks. For dark or extra persistent stains, evenly coat all surfaces with undiluted solution and leave overnight.

STEP FOUR

Mask areas to spray paint or apply metallic paint using a small brush. Remove tape and wipe any dribbles. Allow to dry.

STEP FIVE

Rub all surfaces with a generous amount of natural furniture wax. Repeat as necessary to prevent the wood from drying out.

OMBRE
CABINET
MAKEOVER

Children grow up fast and their furniture needs to move with the times – but that is no reason to toss useful items from childhood if they can be repurposed instead.

Ombre is a French word meaning shaded. An ombre effect blends one colour to another, using tints and shades to move from light to dark.

In painting terms, it is a colour technique that can give furniture extra panache.

MATERIALS USED

Medium grade sandpaper, drop cloths, paint brushes, testpots in a range of tones, waterborne enamel in a neutral, cloths, waterborne varnish, extra drawer knobs (optional).

STEP ONE

Choose a colour range or hue (in this case blue). Use colour charts to select complementary tints (lighter) and shades (darker) within the range. Collect testpots of each colour.

STEP TWO

Remove the drawers, unscrew all handles and lightly sand all paintable surfaces. Wipe clean.

STEP THREE

Paint each drawer front with a testpot, taking care to paint each drawer in the correct order.

Avoid painting along the edges of the drawer runners as this can cause the drawers to stick. Allow to dry and apply second coat.

STEP FOUR

For a hard-wearing finish, apply a top coat to all surfaces, including inside the drawers, with waterborne enamel varnish. Allow to dry before attaching an interesting mix of drawer handles and reassembling the drawers in the correct colour order.

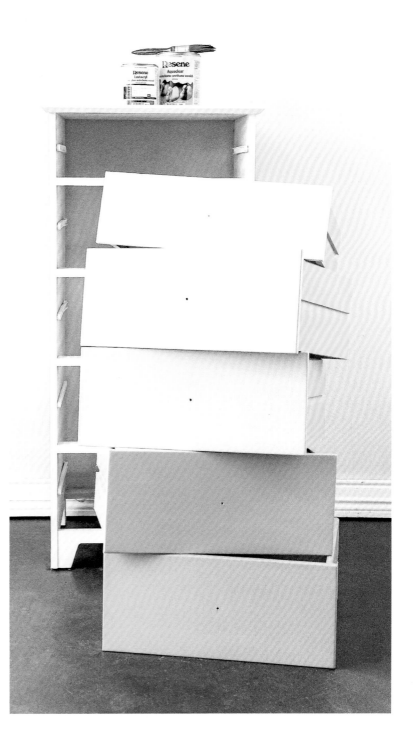

WHEELED COFFEE CABINET

If a cat can have nine lives then so should a useful piece of furniture. It comes down to our ability to consider old pieces in a new way.

A few house shuffles later this tall chest was fitted with caster wheels and given a new purpose in the kitchen as a colourful coffee cart.

See pages 248-250 for project notes.

LEATHER
LOUNGE
SUITE
RESCUE

The sun's daily journey across the sky creates a corresponding daily play of light across the surfaces of everyday household items.

There is something so timeless about the chesterfield style sofa or armchair, with over the top tufting and extra high back and arms.

They carry with them the suggestion of the exclusive club, with the curl of cigar smoke and clink of glass, or perhaps your own private book-lined study.

While there is no official definition of what constitutes a true chesterfield, deep buttoned tufting and a high back and sides are widely considered to be key elements.

The best examples are still handmade in the UK, complete with old-style eight-point, hand-tied, loose-coil springs, and traditional fillings and linings.

Meanwhile the enduring popularity of the classic chesterfield has led to many modern reproductions on the theme, with a more basic internal construction, and including some made with velvet, linen tweed or vinyl rather than traditional leather.

This reproduction leather lounge suite was spied at a favourite local junk shop.

From a distance it looked okay but the sofa had a ripped cushion and an internal frame suffering collapse. The suite's leather was distressed to near exhaustion, see page 59.

The armchair was put out for free removal, no doubt due to the missing buttons and several large rips in one arm.

The only thing was to bring them all home and see what could be done.

Above: Missing buttons and a torn leather arm.

Above left: Repaired and painted, the armchair retains its classic leather look.

Left: Before its makeover, this green leather suite was distressed to the point of exhaustion.

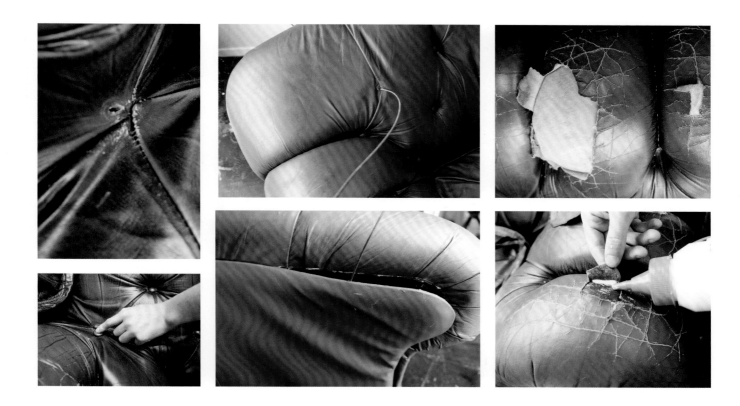

REPLACING BUTTONS

Chesterfields are known for their deep-set buttons. It is fairly straightforward to replace missing buttons, provided you can access the inside of the armchair or sofa.

How this is done and the level of difficulty depends on the construction of each piece.

This armchair's back panel was fastened with staples, which were easily pulled away.

MATERIALS USED

Stiff wire (number 8 gauge), pliers, length of strong nylon cord, upcycled leather buttons, expanding glue, tape, scissors.

STEP ONE

For this project, stiff wire was pushed from the front hole through the chair padding and out the back. Strong nylon cord was attached to the end of the wire using tape. Leather-covered buttons upcycled from an old jacket were attached to the other end of the cord and the wire was pulled back though.

STEP TWO

A spot of glue was put under the button, before the nylon cord was pulled tight and tied to the chair's internal wooden frame.

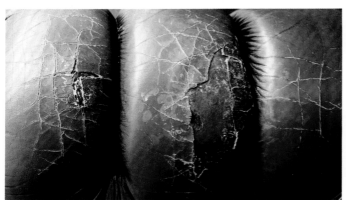

STEP THREE

The back was glued and staples tapped back in. The chair was turned over and weights used to press the glue as it dried.

PATCHING RIPS

The ability to patch a hole is the difference between keeping a chair or dumping it.

MATERIALS USED

Flexible sandable filler, plastic scraper, sandpaper, disposable gloves.

STEP ONE

Cut a leather patch slightly larger than the hole to be fixed. Poke the patch into the hole so that it sits flat.

Squirt builder's glue under the edges and press down. Wipe off any glue with a damp cloth. Press it flat using a plastic bag and heavy weights for approximately 20 minutes.

Remove bag and weights and allow glue to fully dry.

STEP TWO

Squirt out a good dollop of flexible, sandable filler. Use an ice cream container lid or similar flexible plastic to cut a scraper. Use this to smooth the filler out across the entire patched area.

Allow to dry before lightly sanding over the entire patched area, including the edges. You may need to repeat the process of filling and sanding several times to achieve a smooth finish.

STEP THREE

If the patched area looks too smooth add extra texture. Wearing thin disposable gloves, squirt a little filler into one palm. Pat your hands together, then run them carefully over the patched area and adjacent leather. Once dry it can be painted.

Turn to pages 149 for details on painting this armchair.

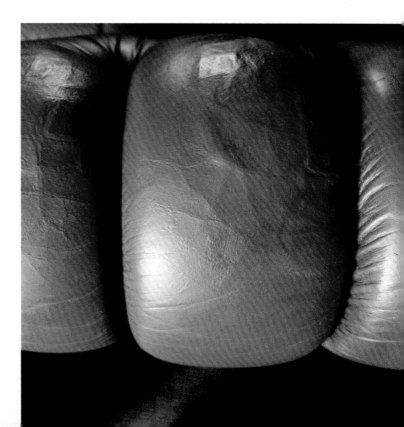

GREEN
LOUNGE
SUITE

This suite needed to be patched in places. In some areas, badly damaged leather was also repaired using flexible filler. The suite required a good clean inside and out as well as some repair work to the internal timber frame. This had broken in places, along with some of the elasticated straps, causing the cushions to sag.

An easy step in the project was the suite's round wooden feet, which were unscrewed and sprayed antique gold.

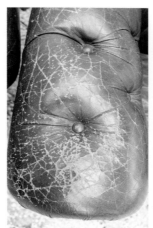

PAINTING LEATHER FURNITURE

MATERIALS USED

Drop cloth, paint brush, cloths, extra water, container for diluting paint, gold paint for feet, low sheen waterborne Lumbersider in a colour of your choosing. See pages 248-250 for project notes.

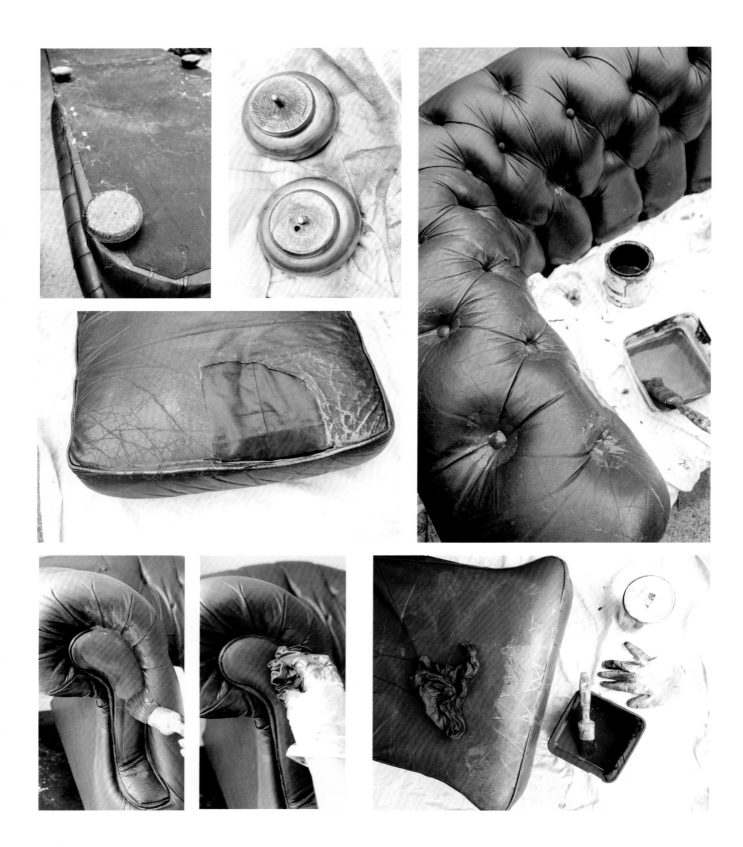

STEP ONE

Ensure the furniture is free of dust, clean and dry. Water the paint down by a ratio of 1:2. Have a jar of water handy for extra dilution, as needed.

STEP TWO

Dab the paint into the deepest crevices with the brush. Dilute the paint with water as necessary to spread thinly over a wide area. Using the gloves and cloth, work the paint into all crevices and wrinkles and over all areas.

Aim to have the paint layer just thick enough to give coverage. Allow the paint to fully dry.

If necessary, gently sand areas to take the paint layer back a little, for instance on the domes, pictured right.

STEP THREE

Turn the chair upside down and paint the feet gold. Allow to fully dry before righting the chair again. Or in the case of the green suite, unscrew the feet and spray paint. Or in the case of the green suite, unscrew the feet and spraypaint. Allow to dry before reattaching.

FLORAL
SOFA
MAKEOVER

Collectively we send millions of tonnes of waste to landfill annually.

In an effort to reduce waste, Refuse Transfer Stations increasingly have second-hand shops operating alongside their facility, where members of the public can drop off items which might otherwise be dumped. Goods are then on-sold to the public at low prices.

As a result, the local dump shop is a place where interesting objects and bargains can be found.

The two-seater sofa (below) was bought at my city dump shop for just $19.

PAINTING A SOFA BASE

The sofa was in perfect condition and could have been used as is, but I decided to go for a lighter, more modern look rather than the loud floral orange.

Upholstery fabric can be painted – for best results choose furniture with a tight weave fabric and no pile.

Paint tends to seep through the threads of loosely woven fabric before it dries.

The surface area of fluffy fabric also means it absorbs a lot of paint and feels stiff when it has dried.

This particular couch was covered in a synthetic velvet with deep tufted pile. The intense pattern and bright colours require thick coats of paint to fully cover the pattern.

For all these reasons, I decided to paint the sofa base and find a matching fabric to recover the squabs.

MATERIALS USED

Drop cloth, old paint brush, paint for 3-4 coats, electric sander and sandpapers, scissors, firm fabric, carpenter's glue, weights, flexible sandable filler.

STEP ONE

Sofas can have nice-looking legs that are covered with an old-fashioned skirt.

These can be simple to remove and doing so changes the look of a sofa or armchair considerably.

The sofa skirt on this couch was attached to the base with staples and was easily pulled off using pliers. Exposing the sofa's simple square legs immediately gave it a more streamlined, lighter appearance.

STEP TWO

Multiple coats of paint are required to cover a strong pattern.

If you have spare waterborne non-gloss paint within close range of your final colour, the first coat is a good opportunity to use it.

Water the paint down by half. Lay drop cloths. Remove the cushions and start painting, using a back and forth motion to really work the paint in.

Apply 1-2 base coats as necessary to cover the pattern. Allow to dry.

STEP THREE

Use an electric sander over the painted areas as necessary to reduce the rough feel of the fabric.

Start with light-medium grade sandpaper, taking care not to damage the fabric. Sanded back, the fabric takes on the appearance and feel of highly textured vinyl or stiff suede.

For high-touch areas such as armrests use a flexible, sandable filler to achieve a smooth feeling surface.

STEP FOUR

Turn the sofa upside down and paint the feet. I used a dark grey. Allow to fully dry.

STEP FIVE

Apply final coat. Allow to dry, then touch up with a spot coat only as necessary.

STEP SIX

Cut a piece of firm fabric 5cm in from the front edge and slightly larger than the sofa base. Reused thermal calico curtain fabric is ideal for this.

Drizzle the base with white carpenter's glue. Spread the fabric out, tucking the extra down into the sides and back.

Press flat while the glue dries. I used books for this.

See page 106 for upholstery details and 248-250 for project notes.

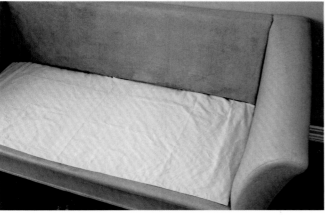

PALLET
BED AND
BEDHEAD

Create a sturdy bed with a distinctive bedhead using basic wooden pallets and boxes.

MATERIALS USED

Various wooden pallets, wooden crates, skill saw, pencil, dropcloths, paintbrushes, paint in several complimentary shades.

STEP ONE

Stack pallets high, wide and long enough to fit your mattress. Trim as necessary, allowing extra length for the bedhead to rest on.

STEP TWO

Lay the dropcloths and paint the base pallets and two wooden crates to use as bedside cabinets. Use a paint that does not require undercoat.

STEP THREE

Some pallets have a solid side which make them ideal for use as a bedhead. Use a pencil to mark the bedhead shape and a skill saw to cut it out.

STEP FOUR

Paint the bedhead with a base tone, such as white. Using two paint colours, lightly paint over the base coat in patches, allowing the layers to blend a little at the edges. Keep working over the whole surface until you are happy with the effect.

See pages 248–250 for project notes.

UPCYCLED BEDSIDE CABINET

This basic bedside cabinet was picked up at a refuse transfer station junk shop for $15 – a great buy considering the cabinet is made from solid pine, is sturdy and has a simple, pleasing shape.

It just needed a paint and some subtle additions to make it more interesting.

MATERIALS USED

Small orbital sander, medium sandpaper, leftover wallpaper, wallpaper paste, drop cloth, paint brush, glue brush, metal ruler, razor-tipped knife.

STEP ONE

The cabinet had previously been sealed with polyurethane, which is not an ideal painting surface. A light sand all over with an electric sander creates a texture the paint can bond with.

It is best to wear a mask for sanding, and to work in an area where you can collect the dust and put it in the rubbish.

STEP TWO

The cabinet was wiped clean using a well wrung out cloth. The cabinet exterior was painted in several coats of waterborne enamel in a neutral shade, allowing each coat to fully dry.

STEP THREE

The inside of the cabinet drawer was painted in a turquoise shade for a surprise pop of colour whenever the drawer is opened.

STEP FOUR

The inside of the shelf was embellished using leftover scraps of a highly patterned pale wallpaper.

CRACKLE EFFECT COFFEE TABLE

This conservatory table was sanded, painted with rust-proof primer, then coated with crackle paint effect and a topcoat of pewter-effect metallic paint. The topcoat reacted with the crackle to create distinctive cracks, revealing the base colour. Once dry, the tabletop was sealed with varnish. See pages 248-250 for project notes.

GREEN-WASHED WARDROBE

Old wooden furniture may not need sanding before a paint effect is applied. A scrub can be sufficient to prepare the surface for painting – or in this case for green-washing.

MATERIALS USED

Drop cloth, metal bowl, stainless steel scourer, paint brush, sugar soap, paint, cloths, gloves, bucket or hose with a high-pressure nozzle.

STEP ONE

Lay drop cloths or locate your item outside on a concrete or other hardy surface. Dilute the sugar soap in a bowl with water in a ratio of 1:5. Wear gloves while using a cloth to coat the solution evenly over all paintable surfaces. Leave for at least five minutes.

Use a stainless steel pot scrubber to rub over all paintable surfaces, in the same direction as the wood grain.

STEP TWO

Use wet cloths and a bucket of water, or a garden hose fitted with a high-pressure nozzle, to quickly rinse down all surfaces without soaking the cabinet. Allow to fully dry.

STEP THREE

Working a small area at a time, paint with a shade of your choice and, while still wet,

rub the painted area back using dry or damp cloths to achieve the look you want. Always work the cloth in the same direction as the wood grain.

You can paint the insides of the drawers, but avoid painting the outer panels as an extra layer of paint can make the drawers difficult to open and close. Allow to fully dry before reassembling.

CHAPTER 3

ROOM REVAMPS

The look of our home, its garden and contents naturally become very familiar to us over time.

This blurring between us and our surroundings is partly what makes the place feel like home to us. The familiarity factor can also make it challenging to see our home with fresh eyes or to identify how a particular aspect of it might be made to function or look better.

Sometimes returning home after time away we're struck by something we have long stopped seeing. Perhaps it's the pleasing curve of a stair rail, the way the light falls in the hallway wall or a photo of baby now grown.

Perhaps it is something less attractive, such as everyday clutter piled in an overlooked corner or tools or materials left behind from a long-abandoned project. Maybe it is an ornament or other object that carries a sad association.

These moments of clarity are worth paying attention to as they can help us to identify the things we might remove or improve.

The basic principles of upcycling can be applied on every scale of our homes; from the tiniest repair job or craft project through to the refurbishment of the entire house.

In essence, upcycling is about using resources creatively. This applies to items we bring home to modify as well as to the things we already own.

Making the most of what we already have is a good place to start. To do this we first need to see clearly what is around us.

One way to look at the familiar in a new way is to think in terms of a series of big and little spaces.

Whatever the size or style of your house, cottage or apartment, each room can be viewed in terms of large or small, structural or intimate.

In a typical lounge, there might be a lounge suite and windows, maybe an entertainment unit or shelves, possibly a fireplace. These are the room's big spaces.

Looking closer you can identify a second tier of spaces – they are smaller and more intimate. For instance, along coffee-table tops, within the alcoves of a shelving unit, and along the top of a mantelpiece.

Unless we are renovation junkies, a room's big spaces tend to stay much the same from year to year. Or at least from season to season. Small spaces, and the things within them, are typically in a constant state of flux. They are the things we rearrange when tidying up and that we switch out when we want to quickly change the look of the room.

Once you identify a rooms' big and little spaces you might become more aware of how well these elements work together.

A few small things clustered about softens a room and adds personality. Too much and it might feel over cluttered and claustrophobic.

Modifying a room's big and little spaces can transform how a room functions and how it feels to enter.

Upcycling can help us to achieve these changes.

UPCYCLED
KITCHEN
SHELVES
AND STOOLS

The kitchen of this city apartment looked boring, and this was made worse by a lack of storage invariably leading to clutter accumulating on the bench, see page 82.

Sometimes the solution really is as simple as adding a decent set of shelves – and the perfect set to use here were a set of old wooden shelves previously removed from a 1960s bungalow.

The upcycled shelves were basic, but made with solid wood, and slightly tapered in shape, making them less overbearing when mounted on the wall.

Before installing the shelves, we painted the walls and added a few rows of butcher block tiles above the benchtop.

Tiles can be relied on to add interesting texture to a wall, and in the kitchen, they create a functional easy-clean surface around the sink and stove.

As this is the first area you see when you step in the front door, changing this space would have a big visual impact on the vibe of the entire room.

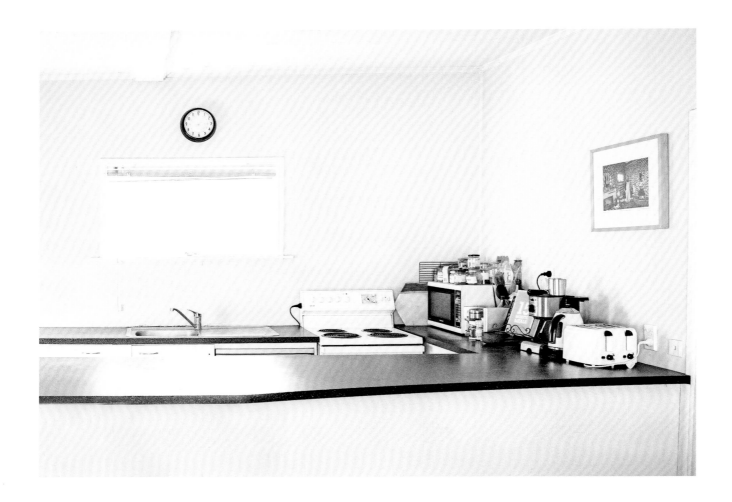

MATERIALS USED

Undercoat for shelves and stools, low sheen waterborne enamel in pink for walls and off-white for shelves and window frame, waterborne enamel for stools and under kitchen bench. Drop cloths, rollers, brushes, tape measure.

STEP ONE

The shelves were sanded, undercoated and painted with waterborne enamel.

STEP TWO

This kitchen leads on to a small open plan lounge, so the wall colour needed to be warm and inviting but not overpower the rest of the room. The chosen shade of pink fits these requirements and compliments the existing dark benchtops.

STEP THREE

Once the painted walls were dry, the upcycled shelves were mounted on the wall using sturdy brackets and filled with an

eclectic mix of kitchenware. Open shelves allow for favourite things to be brought out for everyday use and enjoyment.

STEP FOUR

The dated wooden stools were painted the same colour as the underneath of the kitchen cabinet, to give them a more modern look and reduce visual clutter caused by too many contrasting tones.

UPCYCLED KITCHEN CABINETS

More than 30 years after it was first installed, this brown laminate cabinetry was mostly still in good working order – but style-wise it was well due for a rejig.

One of the kitchen's best features was the vintage marble bench top. This had been specially added when the house was first built, but was now overwhelmed by the brown of the surrounding cabinetry.

In a small kitchen, the easy answer is to go lighter – in this case with a combination of soft moody greys to complement the nautical feel of this simple coastal dwelling.

The deep wall-mounted cabinet was quite imposing and loomed over the bench space, so that was marked to go, as was the range hood that had ceased to work.

Otherwise, rather than tearing anything else out, the aim was to work with what was already there.

MATERIALS USED

Small sander, medium to light sandpapers, drop cloth, paint brushes and mini roller, waterborne adhesive primer, waterborne enamel paint in a variety of neutral shades.

STEP ONE

The overbearingly large wall-mounted cabinet was removed while an upcycled alternative was found. Meanwhile a small sander and medium-grade sandpaper was used all over the cabinetry surfaces to give them a light buffing.

Maximise storage in a small kitchen by separating out special occasion dishes to store or display elsewhere.

Group daily-use dishes in workable stacks, clustering whites together for minimum visual clutter.

All sanded surfaces were wiped over with a well wrung out cloth and all dust cleaned away from the space.

STEP TWO

Because of the laminated surface of the cabinetry, it needed a preparatory base coat to give the paint something to bond to. I used the waterborne adhesive primer Resene Smooth Surface Sealer. This pre-paint product bonds with the laminate surface and provides a suitable base for the topcoat to stick to.

This adhesive primer is best applied using a small roller for a smooth finish.

It is important to allow the product to fully dry. See the project notes for more detail.

STEP THREE

For a hardwearing working finish, all of the kitchen cabinets were painted with a semi-gloss waterborne enamel in a soft grey tone. Allow the first coat to fully dry before sanding away any paint dribbles. Apply a final coat.

STEP FOUR

A small wall cabinet was painted inside and out (see opposite page); another had the door removed to make the shelves easier to access.

STEP FIVE

A replacement wall cabinet was found in the form of a second-hand kitchen shelving unit formerly from a wooden hutch dresser.

It was cleaned, undercoated and topcoated with semi-gloss waterborne enamel and mounted on the wall.

STEP SIX

The back wall of the cabinet was painted with a blue-grey marine effect. This was achieved by block painting with two shades of blue-grey.

Then, while the paint was still wet, the edges were subtly blended in places using a slightly damp paint brush. The key is not to over paint it.

See pages 248-250 for project notes.

An upcycled cabinet provides a stage where collectables and basic kitchen items perform – putting on a daily parade of patterns, contrasting forms, unexpected textures and simple, repeating colours and shapes.

See page 202 for how to make these starfish curios using soda dough and a retro doily imprint.

UNDER THE STAIRS

Clever interior design involves using all the available spaces in your house in an attractive and an effective way.

Sometimes improving a home's functionality is more to do with what you take away than what you add; especially with old houses where seemingly disfiguring features have been added in the past.

That was certainly the situation with this staircase project.

At some point in this old wooden staircase's history someone decided to box in the underneath to create a cupboard.

Judging by the hardboard sheets and plain skirting boards used, this addition was likely to have been added sometime around the 1970s.

Old houses typically lack built-in cupboards so any extra cupboard space is usually a welcome addition. The trouble with this cupboard was that it was long, narrow and excessively gloomy.

Too often things went into the cupboard that weren't easily found again. It had become known by previous house owners as the cupboard of doom.

The solution was to remove the outer cupboard cladding, revealing the original structure of the cavity under the stairs. Doing this also revealed another set of shelves, previously inaccessible in the cupboard's murk.

Once the timber work was tidied up and the original skirting boards restored, the shelves

and inside of the cavity were painted in a deep, moody shade of blue. The surrounding walls were painted in a neutral tone.

Removing the hardboard panels revealed the original hardwood flooring. When the floors were stripped back to show the continuous timber boards, it had the effect of making the narrow hall feel considerably wider and more spacious.

A low corner filled with assorted collectables in silver and mirrored surfaces help reflect soft light into the shadows within.

The addition of a small chair and upcycled reading lamp completed this quirky hallway book nook – creating the perfect spot to sit and flick through cookbooks and other large format coffee table books.

See page 30 for more on the chair makeover and pages 248-250 for project notes.

The colour blue typically suggests attributes such as calmness, order and relaxation. Dark blue tones convey gravitas, adding a depth to an internal space that is rich and warm.

Above: A favourite upcycled lamp, made with timber repurposed from an old bedhead and an upturned preserving jar.
Left: Upcycled fabric bunting and a convex 1930s Deco wall mirror.

UPCYCLED
BATHROOM

A bathroom can be one of the most disruptive and expensive rooms in the house to renovate – including pricey fittings and high labour costs.

Sometimes fundamental problems mean there is nothing for it but to rip everything out and start again, but as soon as you do that you are dealing with the complexities of plumbing, electrics and whatever else is lurking behind the walls and floor. Other times, dramatic results can be achieved through more of a cosmetic makeover.

If your bathroom fittings still function but the overall room looks dated, you can make a big impact by working with what is already there.

The key is to identify which elements must be eliminated and which can be modified, aiming to keep the things to be replaced to a minimum.

This reworked bathroom project shows how much can be achieved with some creative upcycling.

In the original bathroom, the open, tiled shower stall was leaking and draughty – it had to go. The old shower did not make good use of space, so replacing it with a rounded, enclosed shower gave the room a more spacious feel.

The original green tiles looked dated and the excessive use of green on the walls and floor was overwhelming. Ripping up the floor tiles revealed wooden floorboards that needed patching where water had leaked through. The original wall tiles were kept and were prepared for painting.

After necessary repair work was done, the ceiling, walls and wall tiles were all painted. The wooden floor was sanded, whitewashed and sealed.

Two second-hand shelving units were modified and mounted on the walls.

One unit was cut in half from top to bottom, making it sufficiently slim-line to mount it on a wall behind a door. Both cabinets were undercoated and painted with a bright white waterborne enamel.

Painting behind the shelves in green added a punch of colour and interest to an otherwise lackluster corner.

In the updated bathroom, a coffeepot planter sits on an upcycled wooden shelf. Pages from a favourite child's book and band gig posters hang on the walls in revamped frames.

PAINTING
TILES

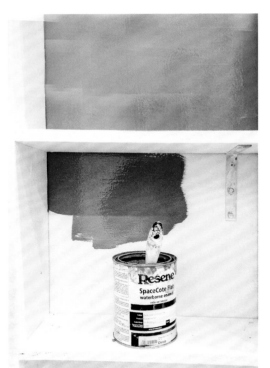

Above: Adding a splash of green to a dull bathroom corner.
Above right: Elsewhere, an old school dentist cabinet is upcycled as a bathroom cabinet.

MATERIALS USED

A small orbital sander and various grades of sandpaper, bleach or other mould killer, sugar soap, scrubbing brush, lint-free rags, a waterborne adhesive primer such as Resene Smooth Surface Sealer, sandable filler, waterborne enamel paint, paint brush, rollers, drop cloth.

STEP ONE

Fill any holes with a sandable filler and allow to dry before sanding smooth. When filling deep holes, the filler will shrink, so you may have to fill these several times.

STEP TWO

Spray any mould. Buff the tiles using the sander and light grade sandpaper. Scrub all surfaces with sugar soap and rinse clean.

STEP THREE

Coat with a waterborne adhesive primer and allow several days to fully dry. Topcoat with water-based enamel paint. Allow to dry. Apply a second coat as required.

See pages 248-250 for project notes.

A restored claw-foot bath, glass lampshade, recycled fireplace tiles and spectacular vintage mirror add character and personality to a modern bathroom. Handmade glass art is perfectly backlit by a set of old louvre window panes. Nooks in the tiled walls house mini arrangements of pottery, retro china and other quirky collectables.

CHAPTER 4

TEXTILE DELIGHTS

There is something very appealing about fabric, bright cotton reels and other bits of sewing paraphernalia – together they suggest so much possibility.

There is also something very pleasing in the process of making things and it is especially gratifying to take fabric and a little thread and turn it into some practical item to enjoy in your home.

A sewing project using second-hand material or fabric remnants or off-cuts offers the extra satisfaction of making something lovely or useful out of nothing very much. You can enjoy the whole experience, knowing that the result will be thrifty, environmentally sound and unique to you.

It is a world away from the waste and pollution of mass manufacturing or the unsafe, unfair work practices that mar the global textile industry.

Even if you don't care much about the ethics of the fashion or consumer goods industry, it is possible that you have at times felt overwhelmed by abundant choices, cheap prices and the seemingly endless churn of mass-produced products for sale at chain stores.

At its worst, modern consumerism is characterised by excessive consumption and a throw-away mentality. It is about as far as you can get from the make-do-and-mend approach of previous generations.

It is disturbing to think about these trends, but it can also motivate us to become more creative and to explore new ways of engaging with material things.

One positive response is to resolve to put our own house in order; to buy less, to care where things are sourced and to invest in quality products that will last the distance.

What happens when we take a second look at things before they are discarded?

Sometimes broken things can be fixed, or someone else can find them valuable.

As fashion designers look for alternative fabric sources, there is a growing trend towards incorporating vintage, retro or post-industrial materials.

Pre-used leather and some vintage fabrics can be better quality than new. Antique tablecloths, retro blankets, pre-loved clothes or furs can all be morphed into something new.

A brilliant example is the old Japanese custom regarding kimono. When too damaged to wear, the kimono is unpicked, mended and remade or sewn into accessories such as bags, brooches and pincushions. This tradition preserves any salvageable beauty from the old kimono and honours the many hours of work that goes into creating each new one.

It might just be sewing but it suggests ways we can live more intentionally and give more meaning and charm to clothing, soft furnishings and other objects we surround ourselves with.

A sewing project using second-hand material or fabric remnants or off-cuts offers the satisfaction of making something lovely or useful out of nothing very much.

ZIP-LESS SQUAB RECOVERING

Cushions and upholstered furniture all need fillers as padding, for softness and form. In our grandparents' day this would likely have been made using some combination of feathers, horsehair, kapok, wool or cotton batting.

With the development of synthetic alternatives such as polyester fibre, sponge rubber and latex have become popular. Flexible polyurethane foam, which was first produced commercially in the 1950s, is still widely used as an upholstery filler.

Whether natural or synthetic there is an environmental cost in creating fillers. They can be difficult to recycle, particularly when made with synthetics.

Recovering pre-used squabs saves money and resources as well as saving the squabs from ending up in landfill.

Here is an easy method for covering squabs that doesn't require a zip. I used a linen colour-matched to the sofa base I had painted, see page 62 for more. Once you have covered a basic square squab you can adapt the method for squabs of varying shapes and size.

MATERIALS USED

Fabric, sewing pins, measuring tape, sewing machine, needle and cotton, scissors.

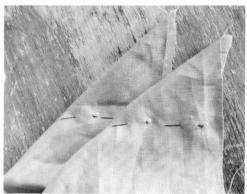

STEP ONE

Remove the old squab covers. Lay a squab out and measure its dimensions, using this as your guide when cutting the fabric to shape.

Cut the fabric to cover one large squab side and the four edges, plus a 3cm seam on all sides.

STEP TWO

Drape the fabric over the squab. Fold the fabric at each corner into a point and pin along the squab edge to shape the corner and side seam (bottom, left). Repeat on all four corners.

STEP THREE

Lift the fabric off the squab to check the corners are even. Removing the pins as you go, sew in straight stitch along the line. Trim the excess fabric to 3cm. Zigzag this edge. Repeat along all four cushion corners.

STEP FOUR

Turn the fabric the right way around and place the sewn shape over the squab to ensure that it fits the cushion well.

Adjust as necessary by taking in the seams a little.

STEP FIVE

Cut another square of fabric to fit the remaining side of the squab, after adding an extra 4cm for folding over at one end.

Putting the right sides of the fabric facing each other, pin the two shapes.

Sew along three seams and partly along each end of the fourth seam, leaving an opening just big enough to squeeze the cushion filling through.

Zigzag along all seams.

STEP SIX

Snip the material at right angles to the edge at the fabric corners to eliminate puckers.

Turn the fabric the right way around again and wriggle the squab into place.

STEP SEVEN

Neatly fold the edges of the opening in together and pin the cushion closed.

Using a needle and cotton and small stitches, sew along the flap to close it up.

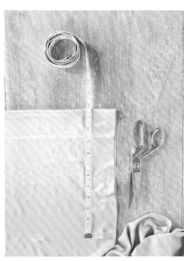

Once you have covered a basic square squab you can adapt the method to recover and reclaim squabs of varying shapes and sizes.

SIMPLE
FRINGE
CUSHION

A frayed trim adds a contemporary edge to this simplest of cushions.

MATERIALS USED

Fabric, cotton, pins, sewing machine, upcycled filling.

STEP ONE

Decide on the size of the cushion you wish to make. If recovering an existing cushion measure that.

Look for natural and loose weave fabrics such as soft linens, cottons and denims, as they fray easily.

For small cushions such as this one you can often use fabric remnants.

STEP TWO

For each cushion cut two squares (or other shape) of the same dimensions, adding 3cm for the frayed edge.

STEP THREE

Put the two pieces together, right sides facing outwards. Measure and pin a line 3cm from the fabric edge.

  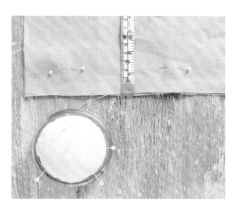

STEP FOUR

Use a fabric scrap to find a wide machine zigzag stitch you like. Sew along all four sides of the pined line, leaving a gap in the middle of one side just large enough to squeeze the filling through.

STEP FIVE

Fill the cushion till firm. See page 249 for more on this.

STEP SIX

Pin along the cushion opening. Push the filling away from this edge and pin a second flattening row.

STEP SEVEN

Slowly zigzag along the pinned line to close the gap.

Starting in the corners, pull threads out up to the sewn edge to create the fringe.

Sewing pattern decoupage:

Decoupage a sturdy cardboard box or wooden crate using brown paper and old sewing patterns. Tear the paper and tissue into pieces and use with white carpenter's glue to cover the box. Perfect for stashing fabric or sewing bits and bobs.

JUMPERS
AND
SWEATERS
INTO
CUSHIONS

Y ou don't have to be a knitter to enjoy cuddly woollen cushions when you can repurpose surplus knitwear into other forms.

MATERIALS USED

Woollen jumper, linen or other fabric remnant, scissors, sewing cotton, pins, sewing machine.

STEP ONE

Sort through your wardrobe for woollens you no longer wear or go hunting at your local charity store or recycle boutique. Match the knitwear with a fabric remnant.

STEP TWO

Lay out the garment and decide the size of the cushion. Depending on the jumper size you may get 2-3 cushions sides from one garment. Handmade woollens can often be unpicked at the seams. If that is not possible, pin a line in the garment where you want to cut. Zigzag either side of this line leaving a gap of about 3cm in between.

Remove the pins and cut between the two lines.

STEP THREE

Lay the woollen square out flat and add any extra woollen panels as needed to fit the size of your intended cushion. Use pins to guide the sewing of straight lines and square corners.

STEP FOUR

Cut two pieces of backing fabric the same size as the woollen square. Take one square of backing fabric and zigzag along one edge. Fold this edge over twice to create a wide flap. Iron flat. Repeat with the second piece of backing fabric.

Lay the woollen square right side up. Place the two pieces of backing fabric on top, right side down, aligning the outer edges with the woollen panel and with the two fabric flaps overlapping generously in the middle. Pin all three pieces together around the edges.

STEP FIVE

Sew along all four sides, removing pins as you go. Zigzag along all four seams. Trim any extra fabric, especially at the corners, taking care not to snip the seams.

STEP SIX

Turn the cushion cover the right way around and ease the cushion inner into place. Trim any loose threads to finish.

Below: Selected upcycled cushions, including one made using the method from page 123.

UPCYCLED
SPONGE
MATTRESS

Curtains, old sheets or large pieces of new fabric can be used, to recover a bed-sized sponge mattress, using the same method as page 106.

Use several large pieces of fabric or sew smaller pieces together for a basic patchwork.

Traditional patchwork uses precise and tiny fabric squares. Alternatively, you can use large squares and fabric strips for a faster result and a simpler look. Two options to consider are squares of all the same dimension or a series of larger squares framed by thin strips.

Choose complementary fabric of a similar weight. Cotton or drill are ideal. Avoid mixing stretch and non-stretch fabrics together.

MATERIALS USED

Sponge rubber mattress, fabric, sewing pins, measuring tape, sewing machine, needle and cotton, scissors, paper and pencil.

STEP ONE

Remove the old mattress cover. Lay the sponge out and measure its top and side dimensions. Write these down and use them as your guide when cutting fabric pieces.

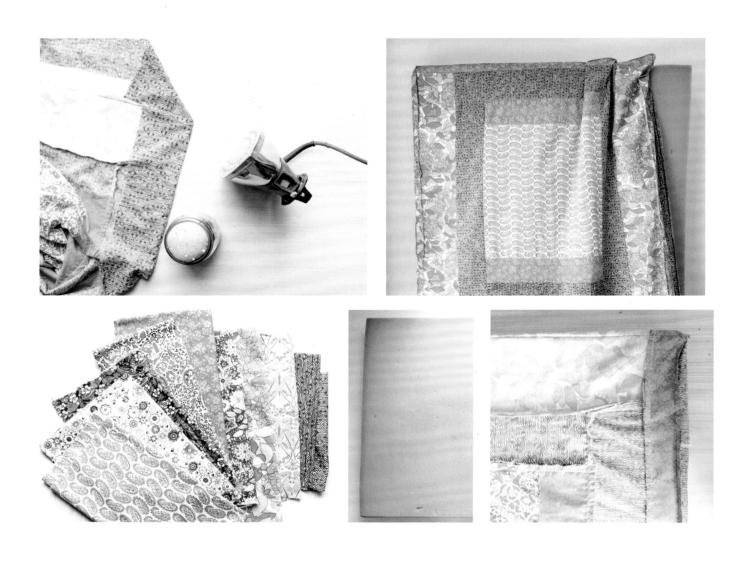

STEP TWO

Cut or tear fabric into pieces and sew together with an overlock stitch, or plain stitch and zigzag, to make a single piece large enough to cover one side of the mattress and the four sides, plus a 2-3cm seam on all four sides.

STEP THREE

Lay the fabric, wrong side up, over the sponge mattress.

Fold the fabric at each corner into a point and pin it along the mattress edge to shape the corner and sides.

STEP FOUR

Lift the fabric off the mattress and check the corners are even. Iron along the edges. Sew along the pinned lines.

   Trim the excess fabric leaving 2-3cm. Zigzag along this edge. Snip the material at right angles to the edge at the corners to eliminate any fabric puckers. Repeat on all four corners.

STEP FIVE

Turn the fabric the right way around and place the sewn shape over the mattress.

   Cut another rectangle of fabric (spare sheets are ideal for this) to fit the remaining mattress side. Add an extra 4cm for a hem along one side. Zigzag along this edge, turn it over by 4cm and iron flat.

STEP SIX

Putting the right sides of the fabric together, pin the two shapes to each other. Use an overlock stitch or plain stitch and zigzag to sew along three seams and partly along each end of the fourth seam, leaving a gap just wide enough to wriggle the mattress in.

   Optional topstitching along the mattress defines its shape (pictured above)

STEP SEVEN

Turn the fabric the right way around again and wriggle the sponge into place inside it. Fold the edges of the opening together and pin closed. Use a needle and cotton to sew along the flap to close it up.

SIMPLE CUSHIONS

A recovered sponge mattress and selection of scatter cushions on a hanging pallet garden bed. Sewn using a selection of classic Liberty Prints from The Fabric Store, thefabricstore.co.nz. See page 240 for more.

Collect a few second-hand cushions of different sizes. Remove the old cushion covers, saving the cushion inner.

Use any fabric left over from the mattress recovering project to sew a matching set of scatter cushions.

MATERIALS USED

Tape measure, scissors, sewing machine, pins, hand sewing needles, thread, paper, pencil, cushion inner, enough fabric to cover each cushion inner.

STEP ONE

Measure the dimensions of each cushion inner and note this down. To each measurement add 2cm to three sides for seams and 4cm along one side as extra fabric for turning.

Iron the fabric flat and cut two pieces of fabric the same size for each cushion, according to the measurements you have calculated.

STEP TWO

Zigzag along one edge of each square. With the right side facing out, fold each of these two edges over by 4cm and iron flat.

Place the two folded edges together with the right sides facing inwards. Pin the two squares together, placing the pins 2cm from the fabric edge.

STEP THREE

Use the pins as a sewing guide. Use an overlock stitch or plain stitch and zigzag to sew along three seams and partly along each end of the fourth seam, leaving an opening just wide enough to squeeze the cushion inner through.

Ease the cushion filler into place.

STEP FOUR

Fold the edges of the opening together and pin closed. Hand stitch along the flap to close it up. Or use the sewing machine to top stitch around the entire cushion edge.

LOOSE SOFA COVERS

A loose cover can be used to reinvent many and various old sofas.

MATERIALS USED

Fabric, cotton, pins, sewing machine, paper, pen, chalk.

STEP ONE

Use unwanted sheets or find a bolt of fabric at an emporium or discount fabric store. The ideal fabric has a subtle pattern, a slight stretch and is at least as wide as the seat of the sofa.

STEP TWO

Make a simple drawing of the sofa, identifying all the shapes. Combine the front of seat area, seat and back of the seat as one shape. Measure the length and width of all areas.

Add an extra 2cm to edges for seams and 4cm to edges that touch the floor. Add the measurements to your drawing. Use this as a guide when cutting out pieces.

STEP THREE

Lay the bolt of cloth on the floor in front of

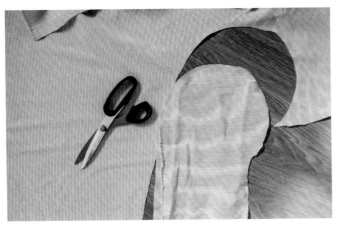

the sofa and unroll the fabric up to the top ridge of the sofa.

Allow enough fabric for a generous crease at the back of the seat area and extra give at the sides. Pin the fabric to the sofa to make sure it is in the correct place and mark with chalk where to cut. Check these markings with your measurements.

If the sofa is wider at the top ridge than your fabric, add an extra panel to each side.

Check against your measurements before cutting. Allow 2cm for seams.

STEP FOUR

Continue until you have cut out all the shapes.

Shaped arm front areas can be a little tricky, so place paper over the front and trace the shape by feeling the edges. Mark it with a pen, cut this out and use it as a pattern.

Remember when cutting out the two arm fronts and the two side panels that these are opposites – you need a left and a right.

STEP FIVE

Put the arm fronts and arm sides together inside out, and pin them together.

Ease the fabric of the arm side around the curve of the arm front. Sew this seam carefully. Turn it right way around to check it sits well, then zigzag the inside edge.

Make small cuts every couple of centimeters on the inside edge of the seam to help the fabric to ease around the curve. Take care not to cut the seam itself.

STEP SIX

Sew the arms to the main front shape. Attach the back panel to the top ridge of the front panel. Join to the sides.

At each stage slip the cover over the sofa to check the fit and adjust as necessary.

STEP SEVEN

Turn the fabric over twice to sew a tidy hem along the bottom edge. Or tack the fabric up and underneath the sofa.

This loose cover has been hemmed and allowed to drape. See page 124 for a loose cover that has been stapled up and under to hold it in place, then matched with a whitewashed table.

TOWELLING
BATHROOM
MAT

Upcycle old towels that are getting tatty but still have some use to offer.

This project involves a bit of hand-sewing which is ideal if you enjoy making something creative while watching a movie or listening to podcasts.

In movie time, this mat took about three movies to sew together.

MATERIALS USED

Two bath towels of similar length, large needle, sewing cotton, scissors, pins, bull clips, rubber band.

STEP ONE

Tear two towels lengthwise into 5cm strips. Using towels of different colours brings out the spiral pattern, or use matching towels for a monotone effect.

STEP TWO

Fold two strips in half lengthwise and use a long needle and doubled cotton to stitch them together securely at one end.

Optional extra step: For a more robust mat, use a sewing machine to zigzag the edges of the folded toweling strips together, making them less prone to fraying.

STEP THREE

Use a bull clip and rubber band to attach the stitched end to a door handle or other fixed object. (If sewing while sitting on the floor you can pin the end down with your toes.)

Keeping the strips folded lengthwise, pull on the two strips and twist them together as tightly as possible to create a cord.

The tighter the fabric is twisted the more robust the mat will be. Pin or bull clip the twisted strips together at the end then stitch this securely. If the towels are not the same length there may be extra at the end to trim.

STEP FOUR

Curl one end of the twisted cord up a little to start the spiral. Use a long needle and doubled thread to stitch it together.

Continue to wind the cord around the spiral, twisting the cord as you go to keep it tight and stitching it securely in place.

Tuck in any loose threads and stitch them down.

STEP FIVE

Continue twisting and sewing until all the towelling strips have been used up or the mat is a size that you are happy with.

Wash the mat gently and lay it flat to dry.

ROUND LEATHER CUSHION

Padded leather cushions made using upcycled leather add comfort to these vintage metal stools. Mass produced in Poland during the Soviet era, these stools are now prized for their simple industrial functionality.
Source: *www.vitrine.co.nz*

Old clothing can sit in our wardrobes and drawers unworn and taking up space, season after season. Alternatively, they can be bagged up and taken to a charity store, or they might be used as raw material and repurposed into something new.

Fabric, leather and vinyl clothing are an often-overlooked source of interesting quality fabric for projects, as with this old leather jacket.

The style of this jacket was dated and unflattering, but the leather was in an attractively worn state – perfect for turning into two round stool cushions.

MATERIALS USED

Sewing machine, unpicker, thick sewing machine needle, thread, sharp scissors, masking tape, strong pins, paper pattern or large round platter, iron, repurposed cushion filling. See page 107 and 249 for more.

STEP ONE

Decide on your cushion shape, in this case a circle.

Use paper to cut a pattern or a shape to trace, such as a round platter.

Identify the parts of the garment to use, avoiding holes or areas such as elbows where the fabric is thin or has been stretched and does not lay flat.

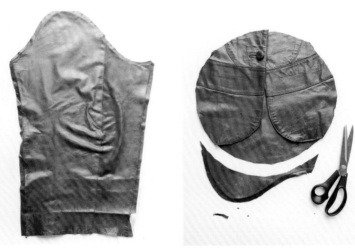

STEP TWO

Unpick the arms and other seams to create more usable fabric. Lay the pieces out flat, wrong side up. Mark the shapes to cut, adding an extra 2-3cm for the hem.

Cut the circles, including extra pieces as necessary to make up four complete circles.

Tape together using masking tape attached to the back side of the leather.

STEP THREE

Sew taped pieces together to complete circles, see bottom image, page 131. Place the circles together, right sides facing inwards, and tape or pin together.

Sew around the circle as marked. Remove the tape and snip around the seam to prevent any puckering, taking care not to cut the seam.

STEP FOUR

Turn the cushion the right way around and press flat. Open the buttoned flap to fill with soft fabric cut into circles, or reuse cushion filling. Tuck the opening in flat and sew around the entire circle to complete.

A VELVET
JACKET
INTO A POUF

A pouf is a round or square seat with no back or sides, that can be used for sitting on, or resting your feet on.

You can make a velvet pouf using an old velvet jacket and a little extra fabric.

MATERIALS USED

Velvet jacket, scissors, pins, approximately ½ metre extra velvet, sewing thread, sewing machine, large sheet of paper, multiple pillow inners, old duvets or other soft materials.

STEP ONE

Identify the parts of the garment to use, avoiding holes or areas such as elbows where the fabric is thin, stretched or does not lay flat.

Unpick the arms and other seams to create more usable fabric.

STEP TWO

Decide on your pouf size, factoring in the jacket size and your extra fabric.

Decide on the diameter you want for the top and bottom circles of the pouf and add 3cm. Draw a circle with this diameter on a large piece of paper. Cut this circle out to make the pattern piece for the pouf's top and bottom.

Decide on the height of the pouf sides and add 3cm to make (A).

Multiply the diameter of the circle pattern by 3.14 and add a 3cm hem to make (B).

(A) x (B) makes a rectangle the same dimensions as the sides of the pouf.

STEP THREE

Cut two circles using the jacket front and back, making sure to include several buttons in the front circle.

STEP FOUR

Lay the remaining pieces out flat, sewing them together as necessary to create fabric you can cut into a number of rectangular panels the length of (A).

The panels can be varying widths but must all be the length of (A). Cut extra fabric panels also the length of (A) in the contrasting velvet.

Sew panels together until the combined width is that of (B). If you want to add a handle, unpick the jacket collar, sew around all sides and attach it at either end across several of the side panels.

STEP FIVE

Bring the (A) edges of the striped rectangle fabric together so that the edges are aligned, with the right sides of the fabric facing in together. Removing pins as you go, sew along the pinned line, leaving a 3cm hem allowance. This fabric loop will be the pouf's sides.

STEP SIX

Pin one circular piece of fabric to the upper edge of the fabric loop, with the right sides of the fabric facing. Sew the circle to the sides, leaving a 3cm seam allowance.

STEP SEVEN

Pin and sew the second circular piece of fabric to the lower edge of the side piece as with step six.

STEP EIGHT

Undo the buttons to turn the pouf right-sides-out, and insert enough filling to make the pouf firm.

CURTAINS REMADE

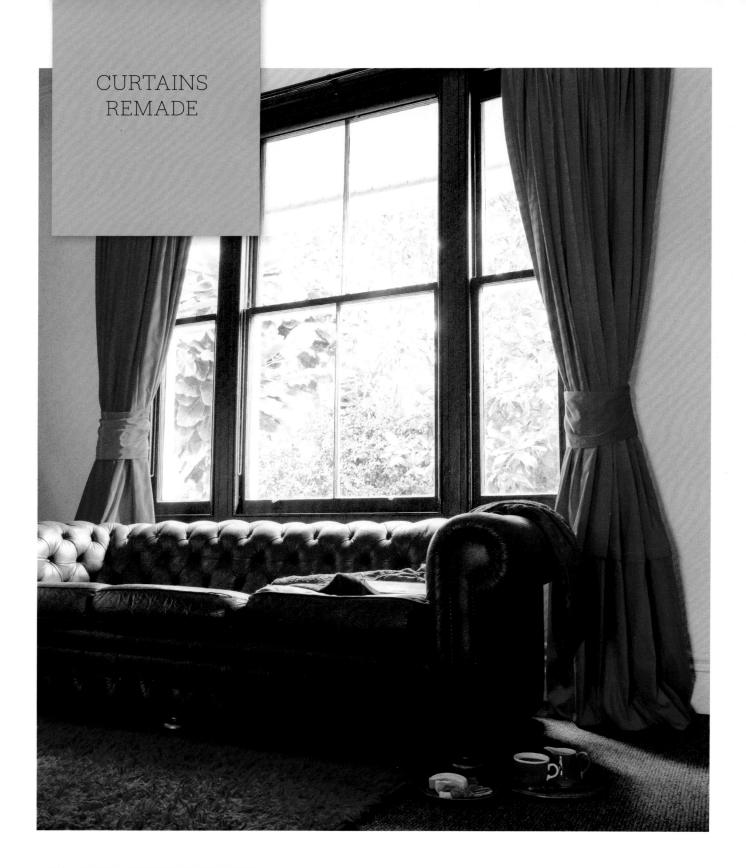

The addition of new curtains can make a dramatic difference to a room's look and feel, with curtain fabric adding warmth, privacy and colour. Taking an upcycling approach to curtains, they can be bought second-hand and adapted to fit a new setting, or sewn from scratch using surplus material from fabric emporiums. Vintage blankets can also be used to add an extra warm layer.

RED CURTAINS

The thick velvet curtains, pictured here, were bought second-hand. They were twice the necessary width for the new window frame, but too short to reach to the floor. The curtains were made the correct length by hanging the first set, and cutting the second set to make up the remaining length to the floor. This extra fabric was attached by sewing the two pieces together so that

the hem sits neatly hidden under the flap of the top curtain. Seams were over-stitched along the front using a close zig-zag stich in red satin thread.

Leftover fabric was used to sew tie-backs and another spare piece of velvet was backed with fake fur material to make a cuddly sofa throw, see page 133.

TWO-TONE CURTAINS

To make the most of a small amount of highly patterned or highly priced curtain fabric, try cutting it into long thin strips and sewing it over the end of curtains made of a more basic material. Small leftover pieces of fabric can be backed with another remnant fabric to make tie-backs. Sew a curtain ring to each end of the tie-back and attach it to the wall using a hook.

You can add an upcycled touch to new curtains by stitching extra fabric onto plain ready-made drapes. The patchwork bedcover, pictured here, was made using a retro padded floral bedcover. It was given

Curtains, duvet and cushions mixing retro and new fabric. Painting on upcycled wood block by Marja Broersen.

a fresh look by combining this fabric with several bright new spotted fabrics. Then a pair of plain ready-made curtains were upcycled to match by adding patches and strips of leftover fabric.

CHAPTER 5

GLORIOUS GLASS

Glass is such a wonderfully useful and tactile material – as pleasant to look at as it is to hold in our hands. It is also able to be upcycled and repurposed in multiple ways.

Glass is made from a mixture of the natural ingredients sand, soda ash and limestone. Its purity makes glass well suited to being recycled.

It is estimated to take more than one million years for glass to decompose, yet glass is 100 percent recyclable and can be melted down and used again and again without any loss of quality.

By contrast, plastic is not truly recyclable. Most plastics are made from the hydrocarbons available in natural gas, oil and coal. Plastic loses integrity with each reuse and is typically downcycled into something less valuable, such as plastic lumber or carpet padding.

Plastic can also pick up the flavour of food it is in contact with and unless it's labelled BPA-free, plastic bottles may seep the potentially hazardous bisphenol A, an endocrine disruptor.

Solid glass, though, is inert. Its non-porous surface does not absorb odours or bacteria. This makes it safe and practical for storing food, including ingredients that are strongly flavoured or acidic.

Glass catches the light and sparkles like water, and its transparency means you can see a jar or container's contents at a glance.

There is something about the feel of glass that makes a dessert look more delicious and a drink taste better.

It is no wonder glass has been used for cups and storage bottles, as well as decoration, since ancient times. It is certainly better than the highly poisonous lead, which was often used for goblets and, some say, contributed to the decline of the Roman aristocracy!

With care, glass can be heated and sterilised. This extends the usefulness of the glass bottles and jars that pass through a typical kitchen.

Often jars just need to be washed and a label soaked off before being put to a new use. For instance, at home we routinely collect small jars for use as drinking glasses or holding individual puddings.

Meanwhile larger jars can be sterilised and used for homemade jams and preserves or simply for sprouting beans.

Heat-safe glass jars and bowls of all sizes can be used for making homemade candles. Meanwhile tiny wine glasses can be glued together to make delicate candlesticks.

Martini glasses can be used as raised dipping dishes and old crystal stacked extravagantly and filled with all manner of party fare.

Extra-large jars can be used as planters and even the smallest cluster of bottles can be used to display cut flowers. For ideas of how glass can find an artful home in your garden see page 221.

For upcyclers, glass is the most versatile and charming medium. It just takes a little imagination.

PRESERVED
LEMONS

Preserved lemons are easy to make, last for months and add bright flavour and colour to dishes.

The lemons are not cooked but pickled in salt and juice. They are a key ingredient in Moroccan and Middle Eastern cuisine.

As with other homemade preserves you can bottle salted lemons in reused jars. Just clean them well and soak the labels off first.

MATERIALS USED

Knife, plate, lidded jars, tongs, lemon squeezer, tablespoon, large pot, hot water, tea towels.

INGREDIENTS

- *Fresh unwaxed lemons*
- *Kitchen salt*

STEP ONE

Check the jar lid insides, making sure that the rubber seals are intact and that there are no nicks in the metal. Wash the jars in hot soapy water.

Rinse and transfer jars and lids into a large pot of water for sterilising. Bring to the boil, then switch off but keep hot.

STEP TWO

Wash the lemons and cut the tips off each end. Quarter each one from the top without cutting all the way through.

STEP THREE

Use tongs to take a hot jar from the pot and place it on a plate. Hold a lemon in the palm of your hand above the plate, open the quarters and push a heaped tablespoonful of salt into the lemon's centre.

Put the lemon in the jar and repeat until the jar is full, with all lemons packed in tightly. For extra-large lemons, use a large jar or cut into chunks and sprinkle well with salt.

STEP FOUR

When the jar is full, add a final sprinkling of salt, plus any juice or salt from the plate. Tap the jar gently to release any air bubbles. Top up with squeezed juice, filling to the jar rim. Use tongs and tea towel to screw on a hot, clean lid. Repeat until all jars are filled or all lemons bottled.

STEP FIVE

One cooled, check the jar lid has sealed. Store in a cool place, shaking the jar several in the first week to encourage any trapped bubbles to rise to the top.

Use after a month. Refrigerate once open.

Use rinds to make lemon zest. Choose a clean upcycled glass jar with a fitting screw lid that has no nicks or scratches. Grate zest from spare lemon rinds and store it in the jar in the freezer, ready for use in baking, salads and marinades.

SELF-
SAUCING
CHOCOLATE
POTS

This never-fail chocolate pudding is delicious, dairy-free and suited to being made in large quantities.

Collect multiple small jars with labels soaked off and use them to make 28-30 self-saucing puddings.

MATERIALS USED

28-30 small glass jars, 2 large shallow oven roasting dishes, large mixing bowl, measuring jug, measuring spoons, skewer, metal sieve and whisk.

INGREDIENTS

- 4½ cups white flour
- 1½ cups cocoa
- 3 teaspoons baking soda
- 2¾ cups sugar
- 1½ cups of light oil
- 3 cups water
- 4 teaspoons vanilla essence
- 3 tablespoons vinegar
- 2 cups almond milk
- ½ cup soft brown sugar

STEP ONE

Preheat the oven to 180°C (350°F). Place the glasses into shallow oven dishes quarter-filled with cold water.

STEP TWO

Sieve the flour, cocoa and baking soda together into in a large bowl, add sugar and mix gently using the whisk. Make a well in the middle of the dry ingredients and pour in the oil, water, vanilla essence and vinegar. Using the whisk, combine everything together gently but thoroughly. Put the mixture into a jug to distribute it evenly between the jars. Mix the almond milk and brown sugar together and pour it evenly over the top of the puddings.

STEP THREE

Place the trays in the oven. Bake for approximately 15 minutes, until the puddings are mostly firm when you insert a skewer.

It is supposed to still be a bit gooey.

STEP FOUR

Serve immediately or place jars on baking trays to cool. Can be served the following day, warmed for 5 minutes before serving.

*Keep a few
upcycled jars
at the ready
for small-batch
jam or chutney
making with
seasonal fruit.*

HANGING
GARDENS

Macramé is an ancient craft using twine and knots that is believed to have dated from Babylonian times. It was used by 13th-century Arab weavers to add fringes to towels and garments. Later sailors used macramé to weave ship ropes and hammocks.

It was big in the 1970s, when owl wall hangings, tasseled string bags and macramé belts, tops, jewellery, sandals and bikinis were all in.

Macramé craft has come back recently as wall hangings, lampshades and simple pot holders like this one.

Make several and fill with herbs and other plants in upcycled jars for your own space-saving hanging garden of Babylon.

MATERIALS USED

Twine or thick string, scissors, tape measure, succulents or small herb plants, small pebbles, coir or sustainably harvested sphagnum moss, potting mix, glass jars with the labels soaked off.

STEP ONE

Cut 12 pieces of twine into 1-metre lengths. Cut another two lengths of 90cm each.

STEP TWO

Gather together the 12 pieces and fold evenly in the middle to form a cord, looped at one end and with loose ends at the other.

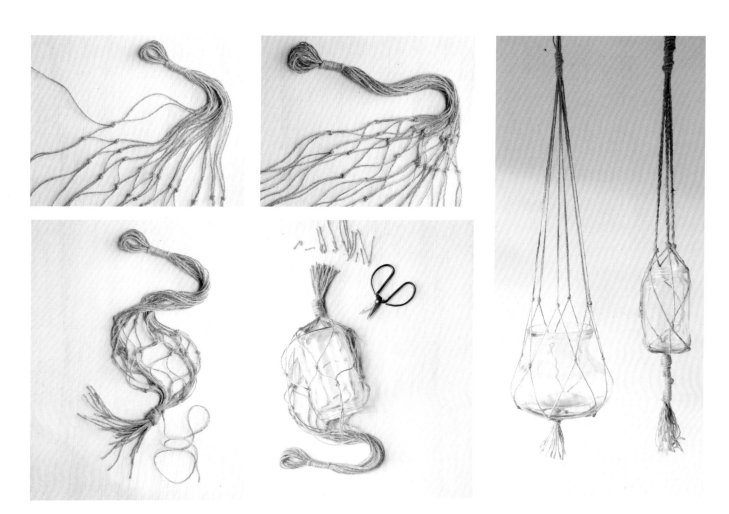

STEP THREE

Lay the looped cord on a flat surface and use one end of a 90cm length to tie a firm knot about 5cm from the top of the loop. Tuck in the loose end of this twine and firmly wind the remaining long end several times around the gathered cord to create a wrapped knot.

Leave just enough twine to tie a tight double knot at the bottom. Use the point of your scissors to poke the loose end up inside the centre of the cord.

STEP FOUR

Spread out the strings and group the 12 lengths of twine into 6 pairs. Tie each pair together using an overhand knot, about two-thirds of the way down the length of the two strings. (An overhand is the basic knot used as the first half of tying up shoes.)

Adjust the knots so that when the lengths are gathered together they are positioned about the same place along the strings.

STEP FIVE

Spread the strings out again. Take one string from a pair and match it with a string from an adjacent pair. Tie these into a second overhand knot approximately 10cm along the string.

Repeat this until every string is knotted together with an adjacent piece of twine.

As with step four, adjust the knots so they all sit at about the same position along the strings.

STEP SIX

Repeat as above, taking care to select an adjacent piece of twine, and tying the knots at the same position along the strings.

Try putting a jar inside the hanger. The larger the jar, the more layers of knots will be needed to hold it securely.

STEP SEVEN

Gather all the loose strings evenly together and tie them into a tight overhand knot. Use the remaining 90cm length to tie a firm knot above the overhand knot and continue, as with step three, to create a wrapped knot over the top. Trim the ends from the bottom of the hanger.

STEP EIGHT

Before inserting the jar in the hanger, layer small pebbles, coir or sphagnum moss and potting mix. Put the plant in and top up around the edges with extra soil.

See page 158 for more detail on plants in jars.

Once you have made a basic hanger, try switching the wrapped knot with a half hitch. This knot ties two strands of thread together and is used in macramé to create horizontal, diagonal and curved lines across a pattern. If you tie a series of half hitches over a central thread they start to form a spiral.

A lark's head knot is often used to start a project. Fold a strand of twine or string in half to form a loop, bring the ends up and around a ring or another thread and through the loop, pulling them to tighten the knot.

A square knot is formed with four strands of twine. The two outer threads cross under and over the inner threads to create a ladder effect.

UPCYCLED GLASS PLANTERS

Adequate drainage is essential for potted plants to stop the roots from becoming waterlogged and rotting.

If your vessel does not have a hole you can drill one using a diamond-cutting drill bit, or fill the bottom quarter with pebbles.

Next add a layer of coir or sustainably sourced sphagnum moss.

Add potting mix and any plants or cuttings.

Top up with more soil, pressed down the sides. Add a little slow release fertiliser or apply later in liquid form. Water well and place in a sunny spot.

Cultivating a garden at a property with an old garden invariably turns you into a bottle collector. Here, a set of shelves originally from a mechanic's workshop makes an ideal cabinet for displaying some of the antique stoneware ink bottles, assorted perfume, junket Rawleighs and other medicine bottles that have come to light over time.

Left: An old kauri school cabinet with its doors removed, displays a selection of vintage ceramics, antique mirrors and assorted French and English collectables.

CHAPTER 6

FRAMING IT UP

There are practical reasons why we put items into frames. Frames protect art from dust, mould and flying bugs. They help solve the problem of how to hang an item on a wall, up out of harm's way.

Putting something in a frame declares we value what is contained within. And while the frame marks a boundary between the object and its surroundings, it is also a window for us to see and appreciate it.

We can use frames to make art from many things – photos, drawings, postcards, paintings, jewellery, pressed flowers, precious scraps of fabric and favourite found objects.

We can use the process of framing something as a way to commemorate moments passed, celebrate achievements and motivate ourselves and others. A guiding criterion of whether to hang something up or not need only be that the item or image pleases or inspires us.

Art and photographs on our walls help tell our story and covey something of our home and our family's identity.

Putting things in frames can also be an important part of the, at times difficult, process of decluttering and of letting go.

When we frame a photo that captures a moment, a treasured child's drawing or other memento, we can put it somewhere for our daily enjoyment. We can then give ourselves permission to get rid of other associated items from that time.

We can curate positive memories just as we choose what photos to display and what to put away.

Not all photos or artworks need to be hung up – large framed pieces can look amazing simply leaning against a wall, and small pictures can be placed along mantelpieces or sideboards.

Frames can also be fashioned from a variety of materials, including basic wood off-cuts. They can be repurposed using previously painted canvases or even shallow painted boxes mounted on a wall.

Some vintage frames are so lovely they can be hung as they are, even with no art inside.

Framing numerous or large pictures can become an expensive exercise, but upcycling provides creative and cost effective ways of repurposing old frames and canvases for new uses.

What matters is getting your treasured photos and mementos out of dark places and onto the walls to be enjoyed.

Opposite page: An image screen printed onto a page from an old French book.

We can use the process of
framing things as a way to
commemorate and preserve a
moment passed, celebrate an
achievement and to motivate
ourselves and others.

UPCYCLED WOOD AND CANVAS FRAMES

Use upcycled wood or canvases to make simple artworks to decorate your walls or use them to create a mood board of inspiring printed images and quotes.

MATERIALS USED

1-2mm thick plywood off cuts or pallet sheets suitable for cutting into squares (15mm x15mm to 35mm x 45mm), hand saw or power saw, electric sander, sheets of sandpaper, beeswax-based furniture oil, cloth, short nails, hammer, twine, scissors, double-sided foam tape or hanging mounts, soft wide paint bush, white crafting or building glue (clear drying), jar, images.

STEP ONE

Ask at your local hardware for spare packing sheets, or hunt for a source of thin timber off cuts, plywood sheets or pallet wood. Cut the sheets into squares slightly larger than your images.

STEP TWO

Sand rough edges and the front surface of each board, following the wood grain with the sanding action. Wipe away any dust.

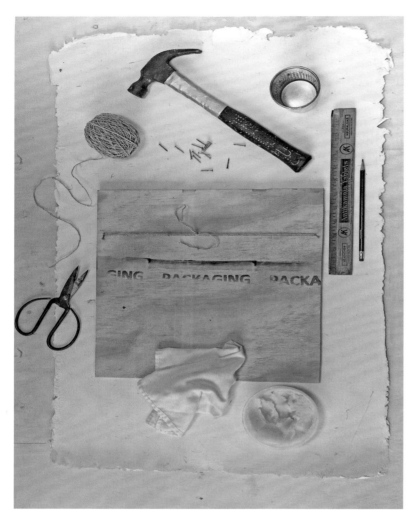

To create layered boards, lay a large board over a smaller one and nail the short nails through the large board into the smaller one underneath.

STEP THREE

Pour white crafting or building glue into a jar and dilute by half with water.

Coat the right side of the board evenly with the thinned glue. Lay the picture down flat and allow to dry before covering the image with a second coat. Use a cloth to give the edges of the boards a light rub with natural furniture polish.

STEP FOUR

Place the board right side down. Tap in nails on either side, an equal distance from the top. Tie a length of twine tightly between the two nails. Flatten the nails down to hang the board flat on the wall.

See pages 248–250 for project notes.

Above: Cover second-hand canvases using white paint, then use the frame as per the instructions in step 3.
Left and below: Cover a second-hand canvas with fabric to create a dramatic wallhanging.

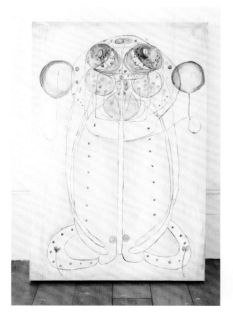

UPCYCLED
PICTURE
FRAMES

Upcycle old picture frames with this step-by-step method.

MATERIALS USED

A picture frame that includes an outer frame, backing board and a mat or mounting board cut to fit, wide brown picture framing tape, glazier points or tiny pins, small pliers and a hammer, nylon line, D-ring or small screws, drop cloth or paper, tea towel, small paint brush, mini paint roller (optional), waterborne enamel for the frame and a flat paint for the mat.

STEP ONE

Disassemble the frame by laying it right side down and removing the back tape and any pins. Look to see how the frame has been put together.

The backing board may be secured with staples, tiny nails or glazier points. Use pliers to gently remove or bend these out of the way.

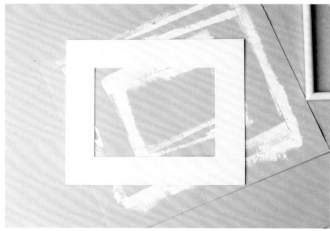

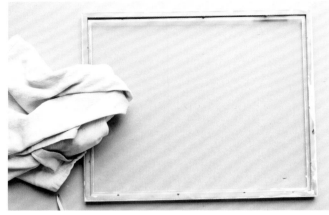

STEP TWO

Carefully remove the glass and wash it with warm soapy water and lay it on a clean tea towel. Polish dry. Wipe the frame free of dust and lay it on the drop cloth.

Coat with enamel paint, making sure to cover all edges that will be visible when the frame is re-hung. Use flat paint on the mat.

A roller is not essential but it makes it easier to get a smooth, flat finish. Allow frame and mat to dry.

STEP THREE

Lay the frame face right side down on a clean, flat surface.

Carefully place the glass back into the frame and check the surface is clean. Place the photo behind the mat and secure using a strip of tape along the top.

Lay the mount right side down on the glass.

Before taping the back up, turn the frame over and closely check that the photo is positioned correctly and that no lint is trapped behind the glass.

Return any glazier points or tiny nails back into the frame to hold the backing board and glass in place, using new ones if necessary.

STEP FOUR

Tape all around the back edge using wide picture tape. On the back of the frame, screw in two small screws or D-ring hangers on either side, an equal distance from the top.

Firmly tie the nylon line between the rings.

Clean any stray fingerprints off the front glass and your picture is ready to hang up.

See pages 248-250 for project notes.

Once you have upcycled a frame and mat, you can apply the method to multiple frames to create a glory wall of awards and certificates.

HANGING
PHOTO
WALL

A simple and lightweight, hanging wall gallery to make.

MATERIALS

20 printed images sized 10cm x 10cm, 20 white square cards 8cm x 8cm, spray adhesive or glue stick, scissors, ruler, a white painted branch or length of dowel, 1m nylon line, white string, four stones.

STEP ONE

Apply a photo filter or adjust the images using an editing tool so they are all a similar tonal range. Or print the photos in sepia or black and white.

Many print stores offer a square print format with white borders, so check for this. Or trim prints to size and mount on slightly larger white card.

STEP TWO

Lay the photos on a large flat surface in vertical columns to form a grid, allowing a 2cm vertical space between each photo.

Arrange the images with a balance of subjects, shapes and colours. Turn each photo over, maintaining the grid arrangement.

STEP THREE

Cut strings the length of each vertical column plus an extra 50cm.

Lay the strings along the middle of each vertical column, with 30cm extra string at the top and 20cm at the bottom. One at a time, lay each white card on clean paper and lightly coat one side with glue. Starting at the top left corner of the grid, place each card, sticky side down, onto the back of each photo, sandwiching the string in between.

Use a ruler to check the cards are evenly spaced on the strings and line up with the photos on either side.

Allow to dry.

STEP FOUR

Tie the nylon line to the stick and hang it on the wall.

Attach a small stone to the bottom of each string. Line up the top photo in each string before tying the string to the stick above.

FRAMED QUOTE

Find a print of an inspirational quote and frame it with an old wooden frame.

MATERIALS USED

Basic wooden frame, with or without glass, inspirational quote printed on plain paper, anaglypta paper or wallpaper, stiff card, spray adhesive, white carpenter paste, small paintbrush, scissors, woodstain, small hammer, 2 tacks, string, book tape.

STEP ONE

Use the woodstain to rub over the old frame. Tap the tacks into each side of the back of the frame.

STEP TWO

Cut the card and anaglypta paper to fit inside the frame. Glue these together.

Carefully cut around the quote. Evenly spray the back of the quote with adhesive and paste it onto the anaglypta paper. Lay flat to dry, then coat all over with the diluted white carpenter paste to form an even seal. Allow to dry.

STEP THREE

Arrange the with anaglypta paper in the frame, facing upwards and with the card behind. Tape it into place using the book tape.

STEP FOUR

Tie the string between the two tacks and hang the picture on the wall.

This quote was hand-scripted by Kaylee Hansen of champagneandchalk.com

PHOTO
GALLERY

Gallery walls can make a dramatic visual impact when well composed. But if a gallery grows over time, and it incorporates several different frames, as ours had done, it can develop a somewhat haphazard arrangement (see above).

The solution was to take everything down and start again – beginning with a makeover of the frames.

MATERIALS USED

Photo frames, dark thread, spirit level, hammer and nails, roll of newsprint or newspaper, picture hanging hooks or adhesive hanging strips, stepladder or stool, Blu-Tack.

STEP ONE

All photos were removed from their frames and both the frames and mats were revamped according to the steps outlined on page 172.

To give the various-sized frames more cohesion they were all painted in black or white and a few in an accent shade of yellow.

STEP TWO

For the uninitiated, composing a gallery wall can seem daunting. Using templates makes this process a lot simpler.

Once your photos have been re-framed, use a roll of newsprint or newspaper to cut a pattern of each one. As you cut each template, write a brief image description and frame colour on the paper. When it comes to arranging them on the wall this will remind you of the orientation of the frame and help you visualise each photo. Sort the templates into piles by size.

STEP THREE

Look carefully at your wall to consider the most pleasing gallery shape.

Photo galleries can be arranged as a simple grid or symmetrically around a large central image.

In a stairwell, you can use a triangular shape to compliment the shape created by the rising stairs.

A gallery needs either vertical or horizontal lines to look ordered, so decide where you want these and mark them out using thread and a spirit level. I started by marking the top and side of a triangle.

Attach the templates to the wall using Blu-Tack so you can move them around as necessary. Start by deciding on the placement of any larger frames and arrange smaller shapes around these until the configuration looks balanced.

Cluster similar sized frames in rows or columns. Ensure accent frames are spread out evenly.

Take your time with this part of the process. If necessary, leave the template on the wall for several days and tweak the arrangement until you are happy with it.

STEP FOUR

Use each template to measure and mark exactly where to attach each picture hook on the wall. Once each photo is hung in place, pull the paper away from behind the frame.

...the blue of Heav...

I'm from Devon

'Lichfi...

CHAPTER 7

LIGHT AND TEXTURE

Lighting is essential for a room to function and it can also be used for ambient effect – tilting the mood from serious to seductive.

Texture, in interior design terms, refers to a material's surface quality. Things that look as though they would be lovely to touch can help a room to feel cosy and to seem more complete.

As with lighting, texture adds an extra dimension that can instantly make a room more appealing.

Curating the interior of your home to create a particular look involves playing with the various elements of design, including line and shape, colour, texture, pattern, proportion and light.

Every surface has a texture, whether smooth or rough, hard or soft. Natural textures can make a space feel more intimate and grounded while shiny or smooth textures can make a room seem lighter, more elegant or more formal.

Textiles such as carpet or rugs, bedspreads, curtains, furniture upholstery, cushions and silky or chunky throws can all be comforting sources of texture.

Texture can be found in architectural elements such as a fireplaces, skirting boards and scotia around windows and doors. Also in displays such as a simple vase of flowers or large pot plant.

Texture comes in visual as well as tactile forms. Visual texture relies on our perception of what a surface might feel

like. It is why visual tricks, such as faux wallpaper, can be so effective.

Understanding how texture works can inform our upcycling decisions.

For instance, you can add visual and actual texture using techniques such as stripping timber back to reveal wood grain, adding decoupage to a smooth tabletop or using crackle or other paint finishes.

By giving an item a rougher surface you can achieve a heavier, warmer or more rustic effect.

Convex mirrors add charm to any space they are put in, while also reflecting some of the room's own style.

Smooth surfaces by comparison can look cooler, lighter and more modern. So instead of stripping a fussy item back to reveal the wood grain you might choose to reduce visual texture by painting it a neutral shade. It all depends on the effect you want to achieve.

Lighting is another factor and is as much fun to play with. Lampshades, candlesticks and homemade candles can all be made using upcycled items, and existing light fittings, as in the case of the chandeliers on page 190, can be modified.

Light can also be bounced into a gloomy corner using large shiny objects or a convex brass mirror. The mirror pictured above was found in a junk store and its brassiness was softened with a dab of black gloss paint, rubbed back.

Lighting illuminates, but it also influences our perception of texture, as do the contrasting surfaces of nearby objects.

Low side lighting, for instance, can enhance the texture of an otherwise innocuous surface, and dark objects will appear lighter when surface texture causes them to bounce light.

Too little texture and a space can feel sterile or boring. Too much and it can be an onslaught for the senses. The fun is in playing around with the elements, experimenting with the extremes and discovering what you like.

CHANDELIER PROJECTS

Having lost its crystals, this black chandelier looked heavy and dull. Switching from black to white gave it a lighter look. Soft wire upcycled from a spiral-bound book was used to attach second-hand bead necklaces.

MATERIALS USED

White aerosol spray paint, plastic beads, perspex crystals, pliers, wire.

STEP ONE

The chandelier was cleaned and bulbs removed before it was sprayed white. Black and fake pearl beads were also sprayed.

STEP TWO

Bendable wire was upcycled from an unwanted spiral-bound book. This was twisted into a series of rings and used to attach the bead chains to the chandelier.

More wire was used to made hanging bead droplets and attached. Bulbs were returned.

UPCYCLED
CANDLES
AND
CANDLEHOLDERS

Fill jars with candle wax and a wick to make your own fragrant candles.

Wrap beads on wire around the jar rims and paint white (see page 194).

Make cone-shaped tea light covers using soda dough. See page 202 for the soda dough recipe.

Apply crackle paint and a white topcoat to a deep vase. Fill one-third with pebbles for drainage and the remainder with flowering plants (see page 194).

You can use repurposed jars, old glass vases – even the inner of a broken coffee plunger to make new candles.

HOMEMADE CANDLES

MATERIALS USED

Wax, large pot, glass jar or vase, wick, scissors, fragrant oil (optional), chopstick, small weighted item.

STEP ONE

Collect candle stubs and wax trimmed from large, half-used candles. Melt the wax in a large pot on low heat until all lumps dissolve.

STEP TWO

Attach a small weight to the wick and hang it in place using a chopstick.

STEP THREE

Allow the wax to cool a little, so the vase doesn't crack. Add a few drops of fragrant oil. Pour it in very slowly. Save a little wax for topping up later. Allow 2-3 hours to set.

STEP FOUR

Add more wax to level the top. Use scissors to trim the wick to just above the wax line.

Warm the pot and wipe it clean using an old cloth.

Later, when the wax has dried, this cloth can be used as a fire-starter.

CANDLE
HOLDERS

Wrap costume jewellery or beads threaded on wire around small glass bottles. Spray paint the bottles and allow to dry. Half fill with tiny pebbles or sand to help hold the candle firm.

For an alternative effect, glue wide glass jars, glass lids and sturdy glasses together in stacks. Paint with a metallic finish paint. Allow to dry.

MATERIALS USED

Glass bottles, beads, wire, expanding glue, pebbles or sand, paint, assorted candles.

Sturdy glass jars and lids are glued together to form stacks. Once dry they can be painted with a drippy and dribbled metallic paint effect. When filled with big candles, these chunky upcycled candlesticks reflect a warm glow.

Dinner party table settings are a chance to play with textures and shapes. Old wine and champagne glasses glued together and used as candlesticks form delicate, twinkling towers.

This hanging candelabra was made from an unwanted purple glass chandelier. Old electrical wires were cut off and a chain was added. It was painted white, and hung up before the old sockets were refilled with candles

MATERIALS USED

Metal chain, waterborne enamel white paint, bolt cutters, candles, pliers, paint brush, drop cloth.

DOILY AND DOUGH CREATIONS

MATERIALS USED

1 cup cornflour (corn starch), 2 cups baking soda (sodium bicarbonate), 1¼ cups cold water, medium-sized pot, rolling pin, fabric doily, wooden spoon, baking paper, rolling pin, clear polyurethane sealer, paint brush.

STEP ONE

Put the dry ingredients in a pot, adding just enough water to mix to a smooth paste. Add remaining liquid. Place on medium heat. Stir the mixture constantly as it warms, bubbles and quickly thickens. Remove from the heat as soon as the liquid has gone and the mixture has thickened.

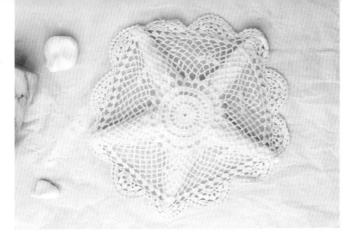

STEP TWO

Scrape the pot sides while the mix is still warm and turn out onto baking paper. Cover with a damp cloth. When just cool enough to touch, squeeze into a ball. Flatten on paper and pinch into shapes. Lay the doily over the shape and press all over with a rolling pin. Peel the doily away to reveal the pattern.

STEP THREE

Lay in a cool place for 5-7 days, depending on the thickness of the shapes. Carefully turn the shapes over as they dry. Or bake at 80°C (175°F). Slow air drying will cause fewer cracks. Broken pieces can be glued with white carpenter's glue.

STEP FOUR

Once dry, seal with varnish. Use as wall hangings or other embellishments.

Transparency and light make this
wide stairwell a perfect spot to enjoy
the repeating patterns and shapes of
this collection of sculpture, vintage
fabric and handmade glass art.

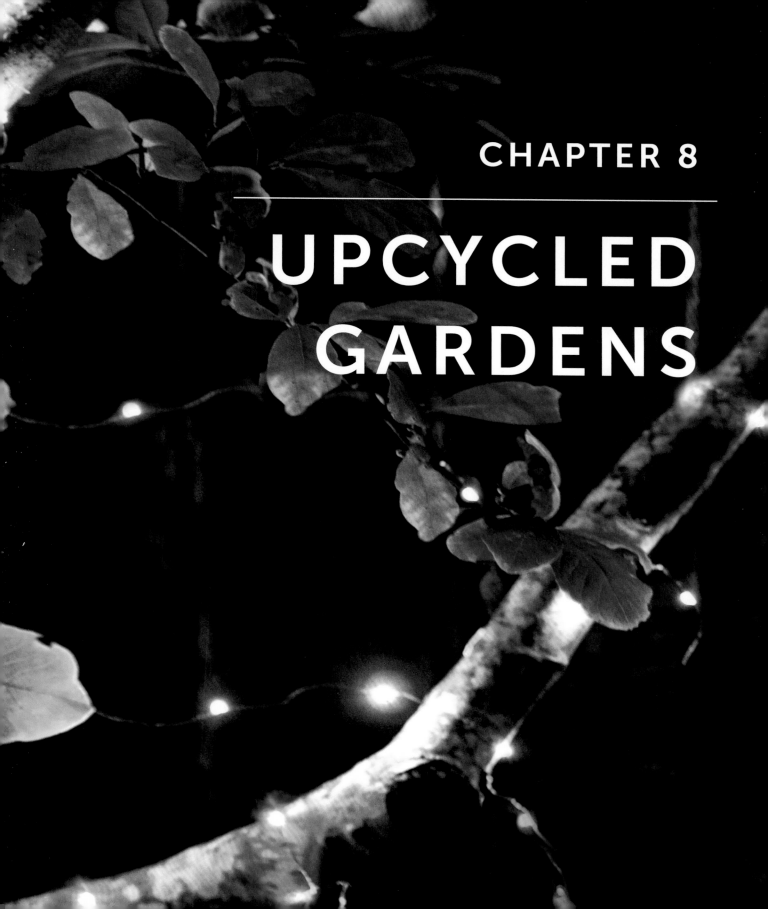

CHAPTER 8

UPCYCLED GARDENS

A multitude of studies confirm what many already intrinsically know to be true – gardening is good for us.

Research in psychology and neuroscience consistently shows that nature is restorative; even brief exposure to nature can improve physical and mental health, improve cognitive functioning, lower stress and blood pressure, even foster greater empathy.

Upcycling in the garden can compound the therapeutic benefits of working outdoors by adding the creative challenge of repurposing salvaged materials and unwanted household objects in practical and attractive ways.

Behavioural research has shown that flowers are also a natural mood moderator, having an immediate impact on happiness and a long term positive effect on mood.

Gardening is a stress buster. Weeding or vigorously digging over a patch of soil is a great way to vent frustration and get some incidental exercise.

Getting out in the garden at the end of a busy day can reduce your stress levels and mental fatigue.

Even a quick dash outdoors as evening falls for a handful of cooking

herbs can provide a momentary respite from the day's stresses.

When we stop to observe some new shoot on a plant, the droplets of water on a cobweb or the movements of insects, gardening can help us to be more mindful and present in that moment.

Gardening at a more relaxed pace can also provide an opportunity to let our thoughts wander, and this can enable our mind slip into a calm, semi-meditative or contemplative state.

Recent analysis of nearly 250 studies found nature-assisted therapy to be effective in treating not only a variety of mental illnesses but also physical pain.

Whether in a large garden, window box or terrarium, plants and soil offer a chance to take care of a living organism, witness growth and see our efforts come to fruition.

Upcycling in the garden adds to this by providing space to play with discarded objects, turning them into something beautiful or useful.

Dilapidated wheelbarrows can become planters and old window sashes can provide tender vegetables with shelter.

Sculpture and objets d'art can coexist happily alongside plants, adding spectacle and surprise.

Dramatic artworks can be made from rusty wire and, in the right places, broken china, mosaics and old mirrors can also find a place.

Whether in a large garden, window box or terrarium, plants and soil offer a chance to take care of a living organism, witness growth and see our efforts come to fruition.

If space allows, an outdoor room can be created to provide a place to relax and better enjoy your garden. If it is welcoming and pleasant to be in it also extends the living and entertaining spaces of your home.

Outdoor rooms can incorporate all manner of repurposed building materials and interior furnishings.

Upcycled garden art can sometimes look a bit hackneyed so it pays to be mindful of using things selectively and artfully to avoid a demolition yard look.

Then again the joy of gardening is also the freedom to creatively experiment and do with the space whatever you fancy at the time.

Clockwise from top left: summer vegetables growing in an upcycled pallet, a lineup of pots are coordinated with a dab of white and green paint while an old length of rope is put to decorative use, upcycled picnic cutlery plant tags.

CORNER GARDEN MAKEOVER

A mossy wall or tangle of plants can sometimes be a delight, but not in this overgrown corner, which looked gloomy and uninviting even on the sunniest day.

Clearing the corner would also create a place for assorted broken ceramics left behind in the garden by potters who lived at the property many years ago.

MATERIALS USED

For the walls: paint scraper, moss and mould killer, concrete primer, 2 x 4 timber length and 4 x 4 off cuts, quick dry undercoat, waterborne exterior paint, roller, large paint brush, garden hose fitted with a high pressure nozzle.

STEP ONE

Flaky residue was scraped off the old wall and the green mould was sprayed. The wall was hosed off and, once dry, it was painted with concrete sealer.

STEP TWO

Old pots and pottery were scrubbed and hosed clean and any broken pieces were glued together.

STEP THREE

An extra timber rail was added to the top of the wall for greater privacy and for training next season's wisteria.

The timber was undercoated and once dry it was painted, together with the wall, using a subtle green topcoat.

The effect of using a light colour on the wall was to dramatically brighten the entire corner.

STEP FOUR

Tangled vines were cut back and weeds removed. Extra soil was added to create a sloping bed and planted out in succulents and clivia. Pottery, crockery and glass garden art was tucked among the plants.

WALL POTS

B roken ceramic pot halves were used as wall planters.

MATERIALS USED

Pot halves, electric drill, 8mm masonry drill bit, 4 x 75mm masonry bolts, spanner, nylon line, chicken wire, hessian sacking, reusable shopping bag, plants, pen, potting mix, exterior paint, paint brush.

STEP ONE

The pot halves were held to the wall. Two drill holes for each pot marked were drilled and screwed into place. The pots were then hung on the bolts and secured with nylon line.

STEP TWO

The pot needed a substantial lining to retain soil and moisture. This was done using wire, hessian and reusable shopping bags.

STEP THREE

The pots were painted with leftover wall paint. Once dry they were planted out with divaricating native plants.

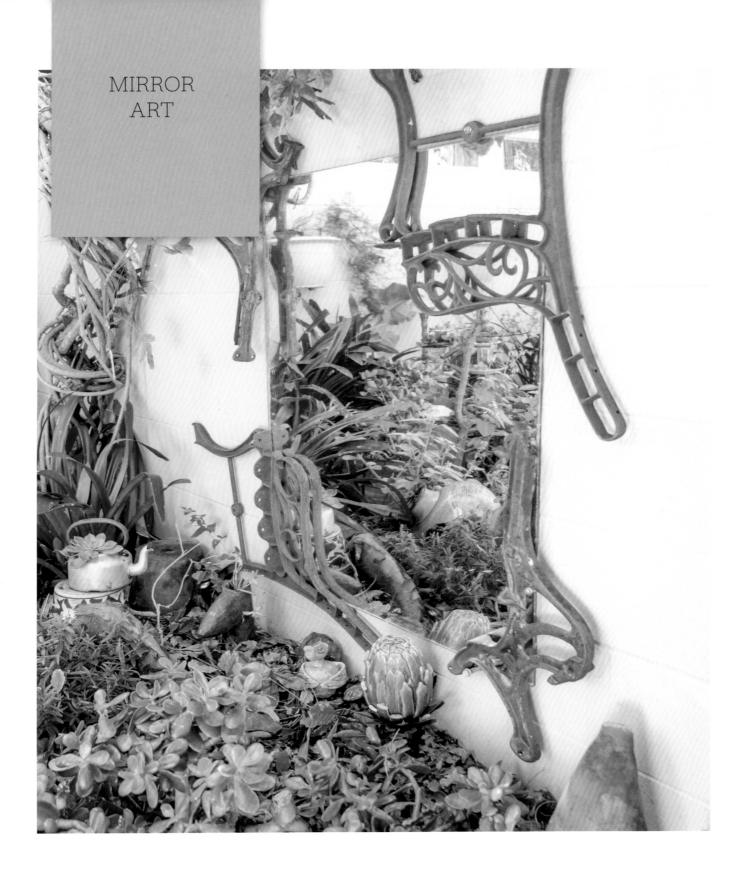

MIRROR
ART

Garden mirrors add light and an illusion of depth to any space.

MATERIALS USED

Large mirror, turps, cloths, bricks, garden bench frame, spanner, electric drill, 12mm masonry bit, 6 x masonry bolts, lubricating oil, all-purpose adhesive, caulking gun.

STEP ONE

Mark on the wall where the mirror is to go. Lay the mirror right side down and apply adhesive using a caulking gun.

Create a waterproof seal by squirting a line of adhesive around the mirror edge and the remainder in even blobs across the back of the mirror.

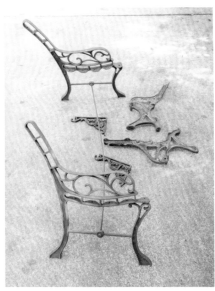

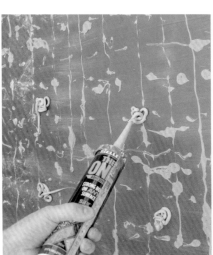

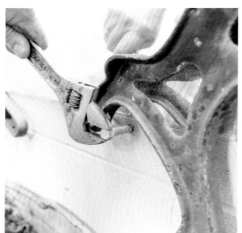

STEP TWO

Firmly press the mirror to the wall. Support the glass with a stack of bricks while the glue dries. Use turps and cloth to wipe away any excess adhesive.

STEP THREE

Lightly rusted steel frames from old bench seats can be found at junk shops and demolition yards.

They make interesting shapes when attached to a garden wall and can create a frame effect around a mirror. Use a spanner to undo any bolts and to separate the various parts of the bench.

Hold the pieces up to the wall to mark where to drill holes. A little oil dribbled onto the bolts makes it easier to screw them in firmly. Attach each steel piece to the wall using several bolts.

GLASS AND CHIPPED CHINA GARDEN ART

A teapot missing a lid, odd teacups, jars and dishes together make a mad hatter's tea party. Glue glass and ceramic items with expanding glue and press together to dry. Fill with tiny plants, pebbles and marbles.

AN UPCYCLED BRICK GARDEN

Gardening offers the satisfaction of taking something ugly or barren and improving it. Even more amazing is when you can use that space to grow something edible.

Originally the site of this raised garden was a sloping, partially paved area mostly covered with weeds.

Chimney bricks add rustic charm to any garden project and can be mortared together to create low walls. They can be bought at demotion yards or at times found for free in skips.

In this case, the bricks were dug up as the site was cleared. String and a spirit level were used to establish the height of the garden edges in a grid of four.

Crushed concrete is recycled from waste concrete and graded for use as hard fill or drainage. Here, concrete paths were poured over a crushed concrete base.

Large pebbles and upturned wine bottles were set into the paths in places.

The garden squares were filled with soil and planted out. Mosaic planters and cloches were added later.

MATERIALS USED

For garden walls: chimney bricks, cement mortar. For paths: sand, crushed concrete, concrete, stones, upcycled wine bottles. Also: garden hose, wheelbarrow, spade, string, spirit level, container mix soil, seedlings.

NEW POTS
FOR OLD

Whether your garden be large or small, pots can be used to grow all manner of plants – fragrant, edible and colorful. Pots add form and enable you to dot flowery splashes about.

After a few seasons outdoors, many pots will be in need of some attention.

Gather up your old pots and transform them with this easy paint technique. Or pick up an assorted second-hand selection and make them into a set.

With unsealed terracotta, a coat of paint also makes them less porous, so plants don't need to be watered so frequently.

MATERIALS USED

Waterborne enamel paint in a white or neutral shade (quantity will vary depending on the number and size of pots to paint), 2-3 testpots in complimentary shades, scrubbing brush and hose, moss and mould killer (optional), 1 large and 3 medium-sized paint brushes, bowl, drop cloth.

STEP ONE

Empty the pots. Save any plants and soil by carefully tipping them onto a spread canvas or transfer them to a wheelbarrow. Keep them happy with shade and water.

STEP TWO

Scrub the pots with soapy water and a stiff brush. If they are mouldy you may want to spray them with moss and mould killer. Rinse and leave to dry.

STEP THREE

Lay out a drop cloth and turn the pots upside down. Starting from the bottom, paint inside and out in a neutral shade of waterborne enamel. Allow to dry.

STEP FOUR

Turn the pot the right way up and set it on an upturned bowl.

Choose a light paint shade and dilute it with just enough water for a wash. Starting about two-thirds up the pot, paint a wavy edge right

around the circumference and down to the pot's base.

STEP FIVE

Choose a mid-tone paint colour and dilute it to a lesser extent than the first paint.

Using a clean brush, paint around the pot again, starting about a paint brush width below the top band of paint.

STEP SIX

Using a third paint brush, the darkest shade of paint and very little water, paint a band around the base. Leave the pot upright to dry, allowing the layers to blend together for a watery dip-dye look.

You can add more paint or wipe with a cloth to try another effect.

See pages 248–250 for project notes.

UPCYCLED WINDOW SASH CLOCHES

A cloche (kl-osh) is a low cover used to protect young plants from the cold. Cloche means 'bell' in French as early cloches were large bell-shaped jars.

Upcycled cloches can be made using old windows, plywood off cuts and second-hand hinges. Our hinges came with some wood in a free bin at a demolition yard.

Cloches can be made to look attractive when painted in a shade that complements your garden.

MATERIALS USED

Wood off cuts (tanalised wood can be used as it will be painted), window sash, 2 x hinges, saw, stainless steel screws, drill, eco cleaner, scrubbing brush, quick dry primer undercoat, waterborne exterior paint.

RAISED CLOCHE

Use timber offcuts to make a cloche with sides and a sloping lid.

STEP ONE

Measure the sash to determine the cloche's final size.

Decide on the position of the hinges and the lid angle, ensuring the two sloping edges match the length of the window sash. Cut the plywood or other timber into four pieces, allowing for a high back and low front, plus the two sloping sides.

STEP TWO

Using your drill and screws, join the four sides together and attach the sash for a hinged lid.

STEP THREE

Prepare and paint as per the A-frame cloche (page 233). Use a dark paint inside for maximum light and heat absorption.

See pages 248-250 for project notes.

SEEDLING TRAYS

Upcycle old baking tins and empty olive tins as seedling and seed-raising trays for use inside your cloche.

Turn the tins upside down and use a battery drill to create a series of drainage holes.

Water your seedlings regularly.

A-FRAME CLOCHE

For an easy cloche, hinge together two similar sized window frames.

STEP ONE

Wash the window sashes with soapy water. Coat any exposed timber with quick dry primer undercoat. Allow to dry.

STEP TWO

Paint with a robust outdoor paint such as Lumbersider.

Locate the cloche at the best angle to catch the sun and block any cold wind. Sit it on low bricks to raise it off damp soil.

Attach netting or add perspex panels at either end during the colder months if greater protection is required.

In an upcycled garden by the sea, plants and driftwood are happily entwined, path edges are marked with weathered ship ropes, washed up coconut husks and the odd mossy boot. Cups and saucers form crazy stacks or are made into bird feeders.
A washed-up boat is filled with salvaged buoys and a lantern rusts in the salty air.

CREATING
AN
OUTDOOR
ROOM

An outdoor room can be created in any number of places; in a courtyard or on an apartment balcony, in a traditional covered veranda, in an old glasshouse, shed or summer house. Or, as above, in a scruffy area set against an ugly block wall.

Garden rooms take many forms but at their most basic they need seating, a sense of enclosure and some protection from the elements. The ideal spot is sunny and sheltered from rain or wind.

Outdoor rooms can incorporate all sorts of repurposed building materials with upcycled furniture and furnishings adding comfort and personality.

The addition of fire and light extends the functionality of the space into the night.

Festoon bulbs draped in strings overhead do not provide shelter but create lovely ambiance and a sense of enclosure. Fire adds light, heat and an irresistible focal point. Attractive upcycled options include sturdy steel braziers made using upcycled tractor wheel parts and washing machine drums.

MATERIALS USED

For concrete surfaces: water blaster, moss and mould killer (optional), concrete primer, large paint brush and roller, waterborne exterior paint. For cane furniture: bucket, detergent, scrubbing brush, gloves, waterborne exterior paint, old large paint brush, paint compressor (optional), drop cloth.

STEP THREE

When painting concrete, start with a coat of concrete primer. Apply one or two coats, allowing at least two hours between coats and 24 hours for the product to cure.

Use a large paint brush and roller to topcoat with waterborne exterior paint.

Be bold with your colour choice; strong wall colours add a dramatic backdrop to any room, indoors or out.

STEP FOUR

Use a bucket of water, an eco-detergent and a scrubbing brush to clean any dust. Rinse and allow to dry. Use strong glue to fix any loose webbing threads in place.

STEP FIVE

Lay down a drop cloth. Cover all cane surfaces, including underneath, with two thick coats of paint. Spray the furniture using a paint compressor or use plenty of paint and dab all over to ensure full coverage. Use an old brush for this.

Allow to dry.

STEP SIX

Set out the furniture in your outdoor room and add accessories such as outdoor cushions, cosy throws, candles, large glass jars and oversized and colourful pot plants.

Elevate plants using pot stands and use waterproof chests or upcycled wire boxes as low tables.

STEP ONE

Define the floor space, either on an existing concrete pad or deck, or by creating one. Compacted crushed concrete, reused pavers or recycled bricks are all options to consider.

Give the area a thorough clean using a water blaster. If you are painting an old concrete wall you may want to first spray it with mould killer.

STEP TWO

An outdoor room needs the suggestion of walls. You may already have an existing wall to work with, such as the side of a building, hedge or balcony railing. Or you can add walls using trellis or fast-growing plants such as bamboo in planters or potted trees.

HANGING GARDEN DAY BED

When the long afternoons of summer arrive and you really want a comfortable spot outdoors that you can head to with a book, a swing pallet bed with colourful squab and cushions could be just what you are looking for.

MATERIALS USED

For the pallet: sturdy wooden pallet, saw, nails, hammer, drill with 15mm drill bit, paint brush, waterborne low sheen enamel paint in a colour of your choosing.

For the timber cross bar: two lengths of 50mm x 100mm timber (when crossed, these need to match diagonal width of pallet), 150mm galvanised bolt, washer and nut, four large nails, three lengths of 10mm rope (total length dependent on the height of the trees). For mattress and cushions, see pages 118-123.

STEP ONE

Measure your mattress against the pallet and mark where you need to cut it down.

Cut the pallet to shape and reinforce edges with the wood offcuts. Drill a 15mm hole through each pallet corner.

STEP TWO

Paint the pallet in a shade that compliments the garden. Allow to dry.

STEP THREE

Drill holes at the ends and centre of your

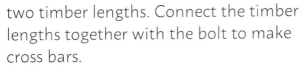

two timber lengths. Connect the timber lengths together with the bolt to make cross bars.

Starting at the top of the pallet, thread one end of a rope though the drilled corner of the pallet.

Tie the end of the rope off with a secure double knot.

STEP FOUR

Measure 3 metres from the top of the pallet and tie a slip knot, (insert a large nail into the middle of the knot to stop the slip knot from slipping). This knot stops the cross bar from sliding down.

Thread the remaining length of rope though one end of the cross bar and back through the hole in the top of the opposite end of that same length of timber.

Allow for enough slack in the rope for it to be raised ½ metre above the crossbar. Tie another slip knot in the rope under the cross bar.

Thread the rope down though the corresponding diagonal corner of the pallet. Ensure that all four lengths of rope are the same between the pallet and the cross bar. Also ensure that the two lengths of rope above the crossbar are the same length.

Tie a double knot under the base of each pallet corner so that the pallet hangs straight. Adjust these as necessary once you have hung the pallet.

STEP FIVE

Take the third length of rope and tie the two lengths above the crossbar together. Throw the other end of this rope over a sturdy branch, hoist the pallet up and secure the third rope firmly. Adjust as necessary.

Add a covered sponge mattress and scattered cushions to finish. Finally, mix yourself a drink, grab a book and head outside for some serious relaxation.

See pages 248-250 for project notes.

If a suspended bed is not to your liking or strong trees are in short supply, you can always mount a pallet on wheels for a land-loving, mobile, garden day bed.

Two wide plastic wheels were repurposed from on old wooden barbecue trolley. The trolley's metal axle was cut in half and used to attach the wheels on either side of the pallet. Two squat legs were made using wood off-cuts and screwed to the other end of the pallet.

A lively coat of pink paint was applied.

Once this had dried, a linen-covered squab was added and a luxurious assortment of cushions and throws completed the ensemble.

Daybed cushions, linen and throw from Bolt of Cloth.

WHEELBARROW HERB GARDEN

An old wheelbarrow is reinvented as a gleaming mobile garden planter.

MATERIALS USED

Electric drill, paint brush, waterborne enamel paint, drop cloth hessian sacking, stones, potting mix, seasonal herbs and flowering plants.

STEP ONE

Roughly sand all surfaces to paint. Wash off dust and spray paint or coat with waterborne enamel.

STEP TWO

Use an electric drill to make drainage holes in the wheelbarrow's curved tray.

Avoid drilling near the corners, as it can weaken the barrow.

STEP THREE

Line with sacking and small stones for drainage. Fill with potting mix and plant out with edibles and flowers.

See pages 248-250 for project notes.

Above: an upcycled tub planter decorated with colourful glass art and architectural salvage items.

GARDEN LANTERNS

Light your garden with easy-to-make upcycled tin lanterns.

MATERIALS USED

Empty clean tin cans (labels soaked off), metallic paint, tea lights, soft wire and wire cutters, undercoat, sand, gaffer tape, felt pen, hammer and nail or an electric drill.

Fill a tin with packed sand. Tape over the top using gaffer tape. Mark a pattern on the outside of the tin using a felt pen. Lay the tin on its side and while holding it secure (I used my feet to do this!) punch or drill a series of holes. Drill two holes at the top of the tin to attach a wire handle. Empty out the sand and wash the tin. Add the handle by looping the wire through the two top holes and twisting the ends to secure.

Coat with waterborne primer undercoat. Once dry, top coat with a metallic paint. When dry, drop a tea light into the bottom of the tin and light it using a long candle.

See pages 248-250 for project notes.

PROJECT NOTES

1 Swamp kauri rolling pin on a bench with upcycled panelling, vintage tea boxes and tins.

4 Glove molds and Crown Lynn swan with assorted vintage items at Flotsam and Jetsam.

12-13 Liberty prints on the hanging garden day bed from The Fabric Store. Retro valve radio, folding tray table and Mid-Century Modern planter all from Retro Addiction.

14 Blue woollen throw, Citta from Good Thing, goodthing.co.nz

24 Vintage clock, lights, Baumann chairs and French cafe chairs at The Vitrine.

28-29 Industrial cabinet from The Vitrine. Jielde two arm oversized desk lamp from Flotsam and Jetsam.

30 Dining chair recovered
Chair back and legs painted with Resene Blast Grey from the Resene Metallic effects range. Seat painted with Resene SpaceCote Flat in Resene Barometer. Black cane side table, stemless glasses and gold candleholder from Good Thing. Reindeer pelt from Gorgeous Creatures, gorgeouscreatures.co.nz

32 Basic carver chair refashioned
Chair painted with Resene Quick Dry Waterborne Primer Undercoat and topcoat of Resene Lustacryl, a semi-gloss waterborne enamel, in Resene Half Dusted Blue. Wallpaper is Pip Studios Spring to Life in Green, available through Resene ColourShops.

36 Painted highback chair
Chair painted with Resene SpaceCote Flat in Resene New Denim Blue, chair legs with waterborne enamel in Resene Nero. Wallpaper Pip Studios Spring to Life in Off-white. Woollen throw and velvet cushions from Good Thing.

38 Sugar soap is a powerful liquid alkaline household cleaner, effective in removing grease and dirt from surfaces. It can be diluted with water or used neat. Active agent sodium carbonate. Avoid contact with skin and dispose of sugar soap water on the ground rather than down a drain as it is harmful to marine life. Also see pages 38, 44 and 72.

42 Mid-century modern makeover Cabinet painted with Resene semi-gloss waterborne enamel in colours, Resene Half Fossil, Resene Ciderhouse and Resene Good Life. Green feathery fern cushion fabric designed by Lisa Baudry for Bolt of Cloth.

48 Ombre cabinet makeover
Cabinet painted with waterborne enamel in Resene Half Thorndon Cream. Drawers painted Resene Carefree, Resene Kumutoto, Resene Hope, Resene Unwind and Resene Whirlwind and sealed with Resene Aquaclear. Wall art by Kaylee Hansen, Champagne and Chalk.

52 Leather armchair and suite rescue
The lounge suite and armchair were all painted using 1 litre of waterborne low sheen Resene Lumbersider in Resene Rustic Red, diluted with water. Feet spray-painted in antique gold.

62 Floral sofa makeover
The sofa base was painted with Resene Lumbersider in Resene Half Duck Egg Blue. Sofa feet were painted with waterborne enamel in Resene Shark.

66 Pallet bed and bedhead
Bed and crates painted with Resene Lumbersider in Resene Half Reservoir. Velvet and linen cushions from Bolt of Cloth. Bedhead painted with Resene Black White diluted with water, and dabs of diluted Resene Unwind and Resene Half Kumutoto.

68 Upcycled bedside cabinet
Cabinet painted with waterborne adhesive primer Resene Smooth Surface Sealer. Topcoat waterborne enamel in Resene Half Fossil and Resene Hope inside the drawer. Wallpaper offcuts Pip Studios Spring to Life Two Tone Off White. Wall art by Deborah Tetlow, deborahtetlow.co.nz.

68 Resene Smooth Surface Sealer is a waterborne adhesive primer that sticks to a variety of smooth surfaces inside or out. Ensure it is fully dry before repainting. Because it is waterborne, it has much lower VOCs than solventborne products traditionally used for this purpose. See pages 84 and 94 for more.

71 Crackle effect coffee table
Distinctive crackle paint finishes can be created using an item's original colour or a basecoat, Resene Crackle and an acrylic topcoat in a contrasting colour to the basecoat. Resene Crackle shrinks causing the acrylic topcoat to crack, revealing the base colour. Sealed with waterborne varnish Resene Aquaclear.

72 Green-washed wardrobe
Wardrobe prepared with Resene Smooth Surface Sealer, then green-washed with Resene waterborne enamel in Resene Glade Green. See page 38 and 44 for more on sugar soap.

80 Upcycled kitchen shelves and stools
Walls painted with Resene SpaceCote Low Sheen waterborne enamel in Resene Blanched Pink. Stools and under the bench painted with Resene SpaceCote Low Sheen waterborne enamel in Resene Cloudy. Windows, door and shelves painted with Resene Lustacryl in Resene Alabaster.

84 Upcycled kitchen cabinets
Kitchen cabinets painted with Resene Smooth Surface Sealer. See pages 68 and 94 for more. Topcoat semi-gloss waterborne enamel Resene Lustacryl in Resene Half Duck Egg Blue and Resene Half Dusted Blue. Wooden shelves undercoated with Resene Quick Dry Primer and topcoated with Resene SpaceCote Low Sheen waterborne enamel in Resene Black White. Cabinet paint effect with Resene Half Duck Egg Blue and Resene Half Dusted Blue.

90 Under the stairs
Book nook inner painted with undercoated with Resene Quick Dry Primer, topcoated with Resene SpaceCote Low Sheen waterborne enamel in Resene Barometer. Walls painted in Resene Carrara.

94 Upcycled bathroom
Tiles prepared with Resene Smooth Surface Sealer, see pages 68 and 84 for more. Topcoated using semi-gloss waterborne enamel Resene Lustacryl in Resene Black White. Wooden shelves undercoated with Resene Quick Dry Primer and topcoated with waterborne enamel in Resene Black White. Towels from Bolt of Cloth.

106 Polyester fibre is commonly used as a fluffy cushion filler. Over time the fibres compact and flatten, but it can be revived and the filling reused. Grasp the fibre ball firmly on either side and stretch the fibres out to create air pockets. Pull all edges of the compacted fibre ball until it has expanded in volume to be double in size with a soft and fluffy texture. Put the edge of larger pieces under your foot and use both hands to firmly pull the opposite edge upwards. See pages 110 and 122.

164 Windowpane painting by Rob Tucker, framed twin baby shoes one of a pair.

168 Upcycled wood and canvas frames
Repaint canvases in a flat matt white such as Resene Quick Dry Primer or Resene Ceiling Paint.

172 Upcycled picture frames
Gloss or matt waterborne enamel in a colour of your choosing for the frame. For free-standing frames that may get knocked, undercoat first with primer. Otherwise a light sand and cleaning the frame before painting is adequate. Use a flat white to repaint picture frames; Resene Quick Dry Primer or Resene Ceiling Paint.

178 Hand-illustrated quote by letterer Kaylee Hansen, champagneandchalk.com.

184 Devonware collectables with found natural objects including a bird's nest.

196-199 Candle holders
Glass and bead candleholders painted with white spraypaint. Flower pot painted with Resene crackle revealing the original gold base through the cracks. Glass candlesticks painted with Resene Pure Pewter from the Resene Metallics and Special Effects Range. See also page 188. Wineglass stacks image by Aimee Carruthers.

208 Vintage glass jars and French botanical wall art from The Vitrine.

213 Corner garden makeover
Prepare walls using the hypochlorite-based wash Resene Moss & Mould Killer. Wear protective clothing. Resene Concrete Primer also seals concrete and similar surfaces ready for topcoating. Apply one to two coats with at least two hours between and 24 hours for the product to cure. Topcoat with Resene Lumbersider in Resene Half Tasman. Mirror glued with All Purpose Silicone Weather-Resistant Sealant.

226 New pots for old
Spray moss or mould with a little Resene Moss & Mould Killer. Wear protective clothing and allow 48 hours before scrubbing or waterblasting surfaces. Terracotta pots can be sealed using Resene Terracotta Sealer. Pots painted in Resene SpaceCote Flat in Resene Cararra for the base and highlight colours; Resene Kumutoto, Resene Dali and Resene Norwester.
230 Upcycled window sash cloches
Protect cloche sashes from the elements with a coat of Resene Quick Dry Undercoat. Topcoat with Resene Lumbersider in Resene Shark and Resene Ciderhouse.

240 Hanging garden day bed
Pallet painted with Resene Lumbersider in the colour Resene Timekeeper.

244 Mobile garden day bed
The pallet bed was painted with Resene Lumbersider in the colour Resene Mozart. The linen pallet mattress covering, throw and linen and velvet cushions from Bolt of Cloth. Dusky Pink Berry Cushions designed by Lisa Baudry.

236 Outdoor room
Walls preped for painting using Resene Moss & Mould Killer and Resene Concrete Sealer. Walls painted in Resene Lumbersider in Resene Timekeeper. Cane furniture painted with Resene Lumbersider in Resene Unwind.

245 Wheelbarrow herb garden
Wheelbarrow painted with Resene Silver Aluminium from the Resene Metallics & Special Effects range.

247 Garden Lanterns
Tins painted with Resene Quick Dry waterborne primer undercoat, then Blast Yellow from the Resene Metallics & Special Effects range. See also page 247.

248-251 Reindeer instore at The Vitrine. Instore at Flotsam and Jetsam.

Material from the following projects were first published in some form in Good magazine, good.net.nz. Dining chair 30, Little Stool 38, Ombre Cabinet 48, Green-washed Wardrobe 72, Upcycled Kitchen 80, Jumpers and Sweaters into Cushions 114, Hanging Gardens xx, Upcycled Glass Planters 158, Upcycled Wood and Canvas Frames 169, Upcycled Picture Frames 172, Hanging Photo Wall 176, Photo Gallery 180, New Pots for Old 226, Upcycled Window Sash Cloches 230, Outdoor Room 236, Hanging Garden Day Bed 240, Garden Lanterns 247. Also images on pages: 22 (centre), 23, 102, 118, 145, 166, 189, 199, 208, 212, 223 Photography Amanda Reelick. Re-used with permission.

RESOURCES

OUT AND ABOUT

Car boot sales, garage or yard sale, not-for-profit stores, street markets, fairs and refuse transfer station stores are all great places to find collectables, vintage wares and items to upcycle. Some pawn shops can also be a place to find quality second-hand tools. Demolition yards are great for salvaged architectural items and assorted building materials.

ONLINE

Online trading sites are ideal when hunting for items of a specific era, style or price. The major sites include UK's Ebay *ebay.co.uk*, the US's Craigslist *craigslist. org*, Australia's Gumtree *gumtree.com.au* and Ebay Australia *ebay.com.au*, and New Zealand's Trade Me *trademe.co.nz* and Neighbourly *neighbourly.co.nz*.

Many websites offer free items, but it is safest to only use local, well-established sites. Community Facebook pages and other closed or locally administered group sites are the best.

Avoid sites requiring you to provide personal details to access free things.

The Freecycle Network, *freecycle.org*, is an international nonprofit network enabling people to swap free items at a local level.

Neighbourly, *neighbourly.co.nz*, is a password protected website allowing New Zealanders to interact on community events and second-hand items to sell or give away.

AUSTRALIA

For a specialist online directory of Australian shops stocking all things vintage, go to Vintage Shops Australia, *vintageshops.com.au*.

The Bower Re-Use and Repair Centre in Marrickville, New South Wales is a not-for-profit co-operative with affordable household and office items, *canterbury.nsw.gov.au*.

Brotherhood of St Laurence is a not-for-profit with stores nationwide *bsl.org.au*.

Lost & Found Market, Brunswick East, Victoria is huge and full of retro and other goods *lostandfoundmarket.com.au*.

The Mitchell Road Antique and Design Centre emporium in Alexandria, NSW, has seventy-plus dealers and a huge range of items, *mitchellroad.wordpress.com*.

Mrs Secondhand in Brunswick, Melbourne, is a very popular store specialising in second-hand furniture and bric-a-brac, *mrssecondhand.com.au*.

Started in 1880 by the Salvation Army, Salvos Stores are a huge network of collection centres and stores, *salvosstores.salvos.org.au*.

Sydney Used Furniture offers furniture and collectables for all budgets. In store at Dulwich Hill and online, *sydneyusedfurniture.com*.

NEW ZEALAND

For a nationwide directory of sustainable businesses and upcycled goods, go to No Brand New, *nobrandnew.com*.

Antique Alley, Auckland, is a tiny store crammed with collectables, *antiquealley.co.nz*.

Arkwrights, Dunedin, includes several vintage and retro stores, *arkwrightsantiquesnz.com*.

Bolt of Cloth, Christchurch, is a go-to place for lovers of colourful, contemporary fabrics, curtains and cushions, *boltofcloth.com*.

A tiny store in Port Chalmers, Box of Birds is full of vintage treasures, *boxofbirds.kiwi.nz*.

Ferry Antique Centre, Christchurch is a collective of five vintage and collectable dealers. See Facebook, FerryAntiqueCentre.

Flotsam and Jetsam, Auckland, has a reliably quirky selection of original pieces and homewares staples, *flotsamandjetsam.co.nz*.

Good Thing is a favourite Auckland homewares store for mixing a bit of new with the retro treasures, *www.goodthing.co.nz*.

Hospice Shops have more than 125 retails stores throughout the country, with a reliably good offering. Their motto: 'Turning second-hand goods into first-class care.' *hospice.org.nz*.

Hunters and Collectors, Wellington, is a destination store for second-hand, designer goods, furniture and more. See Facebook huntersandcollectorswellington.

Junk and Disorderly, Auckland, has a large warehouse of treasures, *junkndisorderly.co.nz*.

Resene Paints is New Zealand's largest privately owned paint manufacturing company with a core ethos of sustainability and innovation and a huge range of quality paint and related products, *resene.co.nz*.

Retro Addiction is a super cute retro and vintage specialty shop, *www.retroaddiction.co.nz*.

The Fabric Store has four stores nationwide for designer fabrics, merino products and numerous Liberty of London prints, *thefabricstore.co.nz*.

The Family Store, the Salvation Army's 125 stores across New Zealand, are great sources of second-hand furniture and goods. See *salvationarmy.org.nz* to find a local store.

The Vitrine, Auckland, has a warehouse of original vintage industrial and antique items from all over Europe, *inthevitrine.com*.

Trade Aid offers online and retail stores nationwide, with quality handmade and fair trade homewares and textiles, *tradeaid.org.nz*.

Vintage Wonderland, Christchurch, is a treasure trove of homewares, tools and more.
See Facebook Vintagewonderlandnz.

ABOUT THE AUTHOR

SARAH HEERINGA

By day, Sarah is an award winning magazine journalist, editor and stylist. By night (and over many weekends), she and her husband have renovated four old houses, using as many found and recycled materials as possible.

Sarah is an avid upcycler and believes that starting with something old or unwanted liberates you to experiment.

She is passionate about the importance of home as a nurturing and creative hub.

As the editor, and now contributing editor, of *Good* magazine, Sarah has created a long-running Resene Makeover series and runs workshops on upcycling. Her book, *Reclaim That: Upcycling your Home with Style* (New Holland 2015), has been sold in six countries and translated into German. *Upcycling with Style* is her second book.

Sarah lives in Auckland with her husband Vincent, two of her four children, animals and a beehive.

Visit *SarahHeeringa.com* for more upcycling projects, recipes and Sarah's blog.

AMANDA REELICK - PHOTOGRAPHER

Amanda is a Kiwi who lives and works as a professional photographer in Auckland, New Zealand. Her magazine editorial work over the past years includes frequent contributions to *Good*, typically in collaboration with Sarah.

See *AmandaReelick.com* for more of Amanda's work.

ACKNOWLEDGEMENTS

Special thanks to Dave Atkins, managing director of ICG for his firm support from the very beginning of this book project. Also to my talented colleagues at ICG and *Good* magazine, where many of these upcycling projects first featured. Thanks to publisher Melissa Gardi, editor Carolyn Enting, also Natalie Cyra and Lisa Lodge.

The photographer Amanda Reelick's contribution to this book has been invaluable and the many hours spent working together on photoshoots have all been enjoyable.

I am very grateful to New Holland publisher Sarah Beresford for encouraging me to write my second book as well as for the input from the wider New Holland team to help make *Upcycling with Style* a reality.

Extra thanks to Karen Warman of Resene Paints for her ongoing backing of my many upcycling projects – and for the fabulous palate of paints and related products put at my disposal.

To my friend and glass artist Jill Goddard and Ian McDonald, for allowing me to photograph inside their beautifully curated home, and the talented letterer Kaylee Hansen of *champagneandchalk.com*, for sharing an illustration.

Thanks to my parents and extended family and friends for your encouragement over the past months, my sisters Deborah Tetlow, Rachel McGlashan, Miriam Jones and Naomi Stacey and friends Lorna Duley, Pamela Freeman, Christine March, Vernon and Isa Rive, Lily and Ilir Mani. Also to Esther Tetlow, Marlon Gentile, Juanita Holden, Letitia Hunter, Rebekah White and Yukari Maeda for being in photoshoots. To Gary the cat and Oscar the dog for photo bombing and company.

Finally, heartfelt thanks and love to Vincent for his humour and unfailing support as a husband and input as a media professional. And thanks to my gorgeous children Levi, Tobias, Theodore and Wilhelmina for your steady encouragement and patience with the long and often disruptive book-making process.

Opposite page: A glorious and extra-long old leather sofa originally from the Poverty Bay Club, Gisborne.

First published in 2018 by New Holland Publishers
London • Sydney • Auckland

131-151 Great Titchfield Street, London WIW 5BB, United Kingdom
1/66 Gibbes Street, Chatswood, NSW 2067, Australia
5/39 Woodside Ave, Northcote, Auckland 0627, New Zealand

newhollandpublishers.com

A catalogue record for this book is available from the National Library of New Zealand.

ISBN 9781869664961

Group Managing Director: Fiona Schultz
Publisher: Sarah Beresford
Project Editor: Rebecca Sutherland
Designer: Sara Lindberg
Production Director: James Mills-Hicks
Printed in China by Easy Fame (Hong Kong) Limited

10 9 8 7 6 5 4 3 2 1

Keep up with New Holland Publishers on Facebook
facebook.com/NewHollandPublishers